# Greeting Cards
# for the first time®

# Greeting Cards
# for the first time®

## Vanessa-Ann

**Sterling Publishing Co., Inc.**
**New York**
A Sterling/Chapelle Book

## Chapelle Ltd.

Jo Packham
Sara Toliver
Cindy Stoeckl

Editor: Karmen Quinney
Graphic Illustrator: Kim Taylor
Editorial Director: Caroll Shreeve
Art Director: Karla Haberstich
Copy Editor: Marilyn Goff
Photography: Kevin Dilley for Hazen Photography
Photo Stylist: Jill Dahlberg
Staff: Burgundy Alleman, Areta Bingham, Ray Cornia, Leslie Farmer, Emily Frandsen, Susan Jorgensen, Barbara Milburn, Lecia Monsen, Desirée Wybrow

**Library of Congress Cataloging-in-Publication Data Available**

10 9 8 7 6 5 4 3

Published by Sterling Publishing Co., Inc.
387 Park Avenue South, New York, NY 10016
©2003 by Chapelle Ltd.
Distributed in Canada by Sterling Publishing
c/o Canadian Manda Group, One Atlantic Avenue, Suite 105
Toronto, Ontario, Canada M6K 3E7
Distributed in Great Britain by Chrysalis Books Group PLC
The Chrysalis Building, Bramley Road, London W10 6SP, England
Distributed in Australia by Capricorn Link (Australia) Pty. Ltd.
P.O. Box 704, Windsor, NSW 2756, Australia
Printed in China
All Rights Reserved

Sterling ISBN 1-4027-0346-5

Due to the limited amount of space available, we must print our patterns at a reduced size in order to give our patrons the maximum number of patterns possible in our publication. We believe the quality of our patterns will compensate for any inconvenience this may cause.

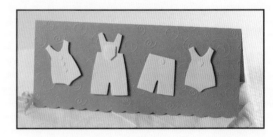

## Write Us

If you have any questions or comments, please contact:
Chapelle, Ltd., Inc.,
P.O. Box 9252, Ogden, UT 84409
(801) 621-2777 • (801) 621-2788 Fax
e-mail: chapelle@chapelleltd.com
web site: chapelleltd.com

# Table of Contents

# Section 3:

## Beyond the Basics—68

# Section 4:

## Dynamic Presentations—102

# Introduction

There are few people in our busy world who don't enjoy receiving a greeting card in the mail, particularly in a smart envelope that begs to be opened and enjoyed in a leisurely sitting.

A card is all the more special when it is handmade with a heartfelt message created with only the receiver in mind. Creating such a card is easier than you may think. With *Greeting Cards for the first time*™ as a guide, your handmade cards can delight your loved ones and bring you hours of creative pleasure.

Although creating some of the more complex cards shown in this book may take some time and practice, there are also many simple yet sophisticated options. We are quite certain that you will be pleased with your very first efforts.

Handcrafting greeting cards can produce so many different and varied results. There are numerous varieties of beautiful papers and embellishments available today which make it possible for you to express your own personality and choose what will best appeal to the receivers of your cards. The latest tools and supplies make assembly a breeze. With such a "custom" look, your greeting cards will be saved and displayed, shared and praised.

## How to use this book

Whether or not you have ever made your own greeting cards in the past, you will soon become an expert by following the instructions provided in this book. The projects herein have been carefully ordered, starting with the most basic techniques and finishing with more-advanced maneuvers. As you complete one project and move on to the next, you will find that the technique you are now working on builds upon that which was taught in a previous project. Should you choose to make a project out of sequence, you may find that you need to review the instructions for the project you skipped. As you master these techniques, your own creative ideas will come to life in fabulous card designs.

Section 1: Greeting Card Basics familiarizes you with the basic tools and supplies you need to begin.

Section 2: Basic Techniques contains instructions for 21 projects that can be made using basic greeting card techniques.

Section 3: Beyond the Basics expands on the techniques learned in Section 2 with 15 additional projects that are a bit more complex.

Section 4: Dynamic Presentations offers creative ideas for packaging your cards, either on their own or together with a coordinating gift, to give them an even more professional appearance.

The purpose of *Greeting Cards for the first time®* is to provide a starting point and to teach basic skills.

The more you practice, the more comfortable you will feel. Allow yourself a reasonable amount of time to complete your first card project—remember this is your first time. You will soon discover that the paper and trim techniques are easy to master.

After you have completed the first few projects, you will be surprised by how quickly you will be able to finish the remaining greeting cards. Take pride in the talents you are developing and the unique and memorable cards that only you can create.

# Section 1: greeting card basics

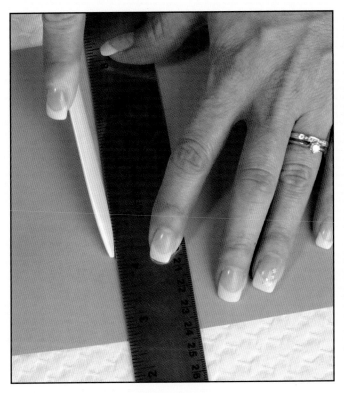

# What do I need to get started?

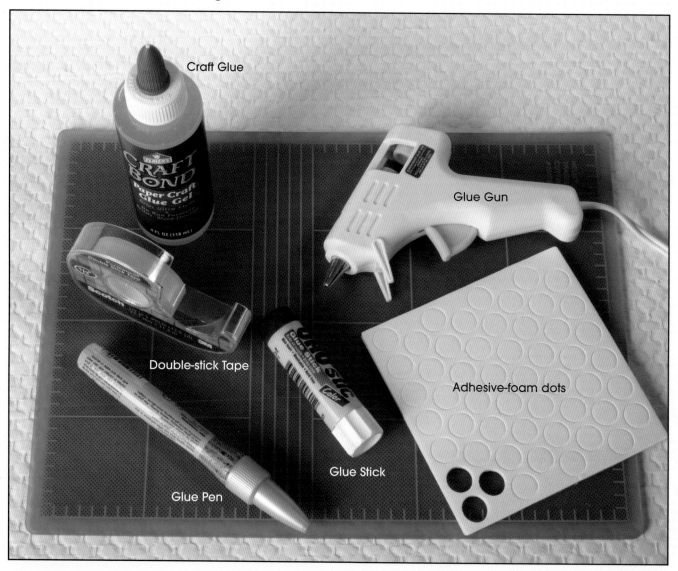

Craft Glue

Glue Gun

Double-stick Tape

Adhesive-foam dots

Glue Stick

Glue Pen

## Adhesives

When considering an adhesive, there is a wide variety of types from which you can choose. Below are brief descriptions of some of the more popular adhesives on the market. You will have the best results using a glue that you are comfortable with and one that is recommended for the materials you are using to create your card.

• Adhesive foam is great to use when you want to lift an embellishment off the surface of the card to create a dimensional effect. This foam is sticky on both sides and comes in a roll similar to tape or in a package of several small individually die-cut pieces. Adhesive foam is most commonly found and used in the form of dots. However, you can use virtually any foam adhesive and cut it to size to suit your project.

• Craft glue is thick and all purpose. It holds light-weight objects in place, is water soluble and flexible, and it dries quickly and clearly. For the best results, apply craft glue with a small paintbrush. Using a paintbrush helps to evenly spread the glue on a desired surface.

- Double-stick tape is transparent and sticky on both sides. It is best used with heavier papers.

- Glue guns and craft-glue sticks are used together to spread glue quickly and evenly across a surface. The glue gun is used to heat-melt and trigger-feed the semisolid glue sticks. The glue is very sticky, sets up quickly, and is best used for attaching heavier objects or those that do not have a flat surface, such as charms or ribbons. There are high-temperature, dual-temperature, and cool-temperature glue guns. They come in a variety of sizes.

- A glue pen is a good choice when you are working with small pieces. The tip of the glue pen is very small, allowing you to get into tight spots without leaving excess glue on the paper. Glue pens are available with roller-ball or chiseled tips.

- A paper-glue stick provides an adhesive that is very sticky, which allows for a quick bond. They are best used with papers and lightweight objects. A glue stick is very convenient and easy to use. However, make certain that you are always using a moist glue stick, as they tend to dry out quickly. A glue stick is similar to a lip balm or stick deodorant in that you turn the base of the container to raise the product up to the top.

## Bone Folder

This tool has a rounded point at one end and rounded edges at the opposite end and along the sides. The point is used with a ruler to form a creasing line for folding cards. The rounded edges are used for burnishing folds and flat glued-on elements.

## Ruler

A ruler is essential for making your greeting card the right size. It is also used for lining up design elements and necessary as a straightedge for cutting and tearing papers and forming a creasing line. A ruler with a metal edge works best.

## Cutting Tools

If you are cutting your cards to size, rather than using premade card blanks, it is important to measure carefully and cut evenly. Otherwise, your edges will not line up when the card is folded. Keep in mind the carpenter's mantra: Measure twice and cut only once.

- A craft knife can be used in combination with a ruler. When

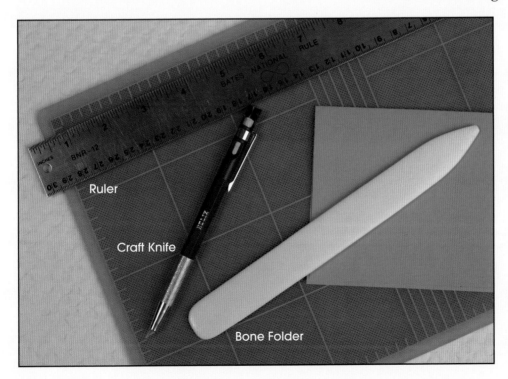

Ruler

Craft Knife

Bone Folder

using a craft knife, make certain to use a self-healing cutting mat or thick piece of cardboard under the paper to protect your work surface.

- Craft scissors are used to cut paper. There are many different models from which you can choose. Some have an ergonomic design that is meant to help keep your hands from tiring. For the projects in this book, look for a pair of craft scissors with relatively short blades and a fine point, as these features facilitate making small, intricate cuts.

- Decorative-edged scissors are scissors that have unique edges, which make fancy cuts instead of straight ones. Decorative-edged scissors come in a variety of edge patterns from simple scallops to lacy Victorian. Decorative-edged scissors are used to enhance the edges and corners of paper motifs, mats, photographs, and cards.

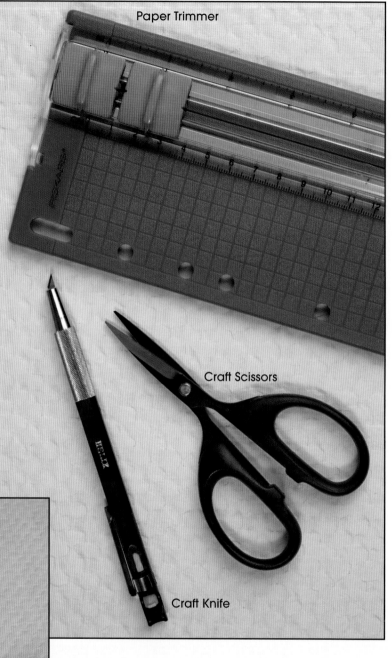

Paper Trimmer

Craft Scissors

Craft Knife

Decorative-edged Scissors

- Paper trimmers are now available in smaller, more-portable sizes. Some have a cutting arm and others have a sliding blade. Which one you choose is a matter of personal preference. Each provides a smooth movement of the blade, ensuring a straight cut. Most paper trimmers have markings for inches and millimeters along the cutting edge and across the body of the cutter, allowing you to determine the exact measurements of your card.

## Lettering & Pens

Lettering can consist of computer-generated letters, handwritten letters, pressed-on letters, or sticker letters.

There are all sorts of pens and markers from which you can choose to get the effect you are looking for.

If you choose to use handwritten lettering, lightly write the lettering style on the card with a pencil or disappearing marker first to make certain your placement is as you would like it, then go over the lettering with a pen or marker. Keep letter spacing even and consistent for a more unified appearance.

## Papers

Choices of paper have never been greater. From handmade paper to paper created for scrapbooking, paper is available in what seems like an endless variety of sizes, colors, patterns, textures, and weights. Use these varieties to help create themes and moods.

• Cardstock is more rigid than paper. It is available in a wide variety of colors and patterns. Cardstock is also available in matte (not shiny) and glossy finishes. You will find cardstock either in bulk packages or in individual sheets at craft, stationery, and scrapbooking stores.

You can also find cardstock that is already packaged in card form. These premade cards are a great choice for the greeting card beginner because they come in a variety of sizes and colors and are ready to use. Matching or coordinating envelopes are usually included in these packages so that all you have to do is embellish the card, using the techniques you have learned and combined with your own personal style.

• Plain-colored paper is available in a wide range of colors and weights. Just as with cardstock, you also can purchase colored paper in bulk packages or by the individual sheet.

Cardstock / Plain-colored Paper

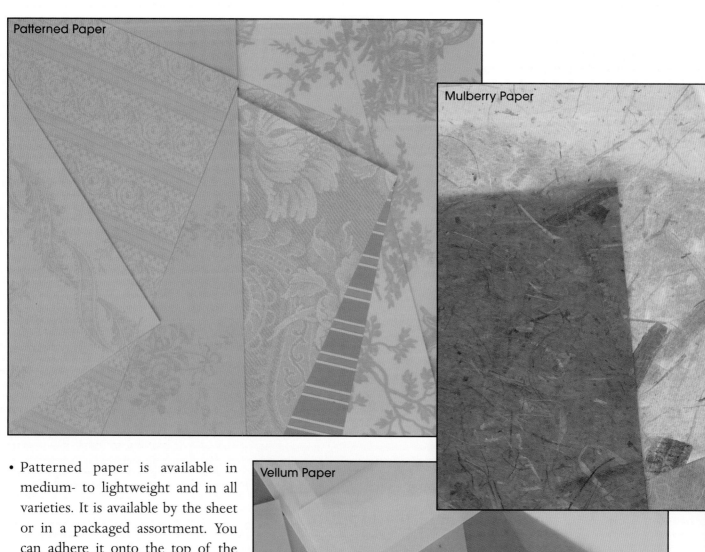

**Patterned Paper**

**Mulberry Paper**

**Vellum Paper**

- Patterned paper is available in medium- to lightweight and in all varieties. It is available by the sheet or in a packaged assortment. You can adhere it onto the top of the cardstock to create contrast or use it to complement other decorative elements on the card.

- Vellum is a very smooth, translucent paper. It comes in both text weight and cardstock weight. It is also available in a variety of colors and textures. Vellum allows elements on the card to be visible through a filmy layer of paper.

- Mulberry paper is a soft, highly-textured paper made from the bark of mulberry trees. Mulberry paper is available in a wide variety of colors. This type of paper is desirable for use on cards because it leaves a feathery edge when you use a special technique to tear it.

## Envelopes

Whether your card will be sent through the mail or secretly left under a pillow, the presentation is more dynamic if the card is housed in an envelope.

If you are planning to make an odd-sized card or one that requires special packaging, you can make your own envelopes, using the patterns that are provided in this book.

There are a variety of materials that can be used to make envelopes, including paper, cardstock, vellum, construction paper, magazine pages, and even fabric.

Once you have determined the material that will be used for making the envelope, measure the width and height of your closed greeting card. Add ½" to both measurements. For example, if the card measures 4" x 6" when it is closed, the envelope should measure 4½" x 6½" when it is folded and closed.

If you would prefer to use purchased envelopes, select the envelope you want to use *before* you begin crafting your card and apply the ½" rule in reverse to your card. Purchased envelopes come in a variety of colors, shapes, sizes, and textures.

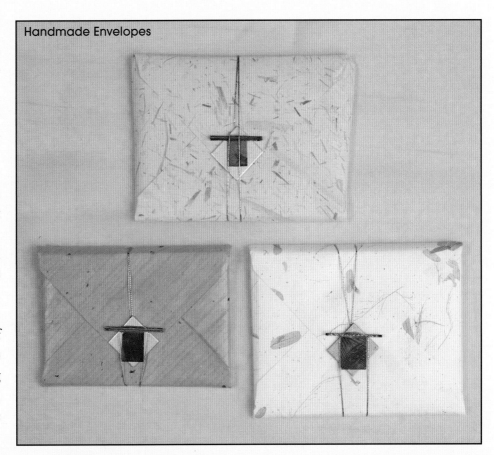
Handmade Envelopes

Purchased Envelopes

Self-mailing envelopes are also available on the market. These premade envelopes actually serve as both the envelope and the card. Additional envelopes of this type are shown on page 109. These envelope samples were provided for this book by Envelopments, Inc.®

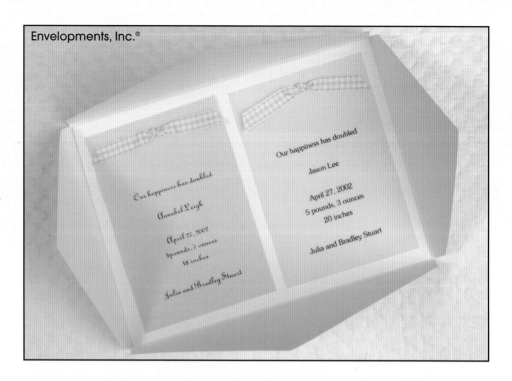

Envelopments, Inc.®

Our happiness has doubled
Annabel Leigh
April 27, 2002
4 pounds, 7 ounces
18 inches
Julia and Bradley Stuart

Our happiness has doubled
Jason Lee
April 27, 2002
5 pounds, 3 ounces
20 inches
Julia and Bradley Stuart

# How do I fold cardstock?

Single-fold cards are the simplest cards to make. They can open from side to side or from bottom to top and can be made any size desired. It is important to know how to properly fold the cardstock.

Using a ruler and pencil, measure and mark the fold line on inside of card. Place the ruler along the fold line and gently run the pointed end of the bone folder down the ruler's edge. This will give you the creasing line. Fold the card over and smooth, or burnish, the crease with the side edge of the bone folder.

If you use this method for all your folds, your card edges should line up evenly when closed. Remember, it is important to start with a piece of cardstock that has been carefully measured and cut with even edges.

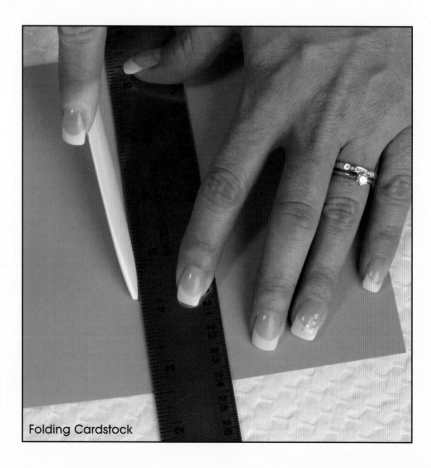

Folding Cardstock

# What else should I know about making greeting cards?

## Helpful Hints

Be aware that substitution is always possible. Replace primary colors with pastels. Substitute patterned cardstock for plain cardstock. Trade star stickers for heart stickers. Make each project as personal as possible by selecting the products, styles, and themes that are favorites of either the card maker or the card recipient.

When you are planning your card composition, keep in mind that it is good to have an element that slightly overlaps another element. Both elements should be clearly visible, but a slight overlap helps to keep the composition from looking too rigid or too symmetrical.

Know when to stop. Usually the best design is deceivingly simple and clean. Too much activity in the design will only be confusing and is not as appealing as a sharp clean look.

Photo Cards

Remember the third dimension. Cards need not be limited to a flat surface. Elements can pop up or hang down for a very special effect.

Remember that you have the perfect material right in your photograph album to personalize many cards. Copy favorite photographs and save your originals. Color-copy machines and duplicate-photograph machines are readily available, making copying a simple task.

Multiple mats are a quick-and-easy way to add bright color and detail to any card. A thin line or border drawn with a pen and ruler can enhance a multiple mat.

Keep supplies organized and at hand so you can grab a few minutes here and there to work on cards.

Try to set aside some time on a consistent basis for card creation. If a given time is scheduled, you are more likely to get to it.

Keep a pocket notebook and jot down notes for future cards, then store them with your supplies. Note which cards you have sent to whom to avoid sending a similar card in the future.

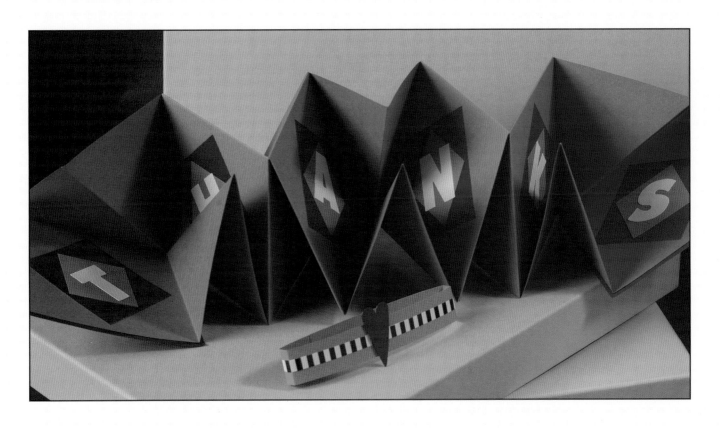

# Section 2: basic techniques

# How do I make and embellish a basic card?

## What you need to get started:

Papers:
Cardstock:
  periwinkle (4¾" x 6");
  poppy (9½" x 6")

Other Materials and Tools:
Bone folder
Craft scissors
Fabric flower appliqués:
  large (1); small (3)
Glue stick
Ruler

Cheerful flower appliqués are used to make this quick and easy card. Details as simple as cutting out a corner make a big difference in the card's appearance. The inside of the card looks as nice as the outside and provides enough room to write a lovely message.

## Basic Embellished Card

*Designed by Jill Dahlberg for Vanessa-Ann Collection*

### Here's how:

1. Using bone folder, fold poppy cardstock in half to form 4¾" x 6" card. Refer to How do I fold cardstock? on page 18.

2. Cut 2¼" square from the top-right corner of card front.

3. Glue periwinkle cardstock onto inside-right of card.

4. Glue the large flower appliqué onto periwinkle "corner" and the three small flower appliqués along the bottom-front of card.

# How do I design a card, using different patterned papers?

There are thousands of patterned papers available that are designed to be "mixed and matched." This card coordinates a striped pattern with a charming French toile print in the same color palette. The added cord gives the illusion of framed artwork.

## Patterned Paper Card

*Designed by Jill Dahlberg for Vanessa-Ann Collection*

### Here's how:

1. Using bone folder, fold cardstock in half to form 6½" x 5" card. Refer to How do I fold cardstock? on page 18.

2. Center and mount striped paper onto front of card with double-stick tape. Repeat for scene.

3. Measure and cut the cord to create a border around the scene. Using glue pen, adhere the cord around edges of scene.

4. Using glue gun, adhere a ribbon flower onto top of cord.

## What you need to get started:

**Papers:**
Cardstock: white (10" x 6½")
Patterned: scene (5" x 3½");
 striped (6" x 4½")

**Other Materials and Tools:**
Bone folder
Cord: cream (20")
Craft scissors
Double-stick tape
Glue pen
Hot-glue gun and glue sticks
Ribbon flower: cream with
 pearl center
Ruler

## What you need to get started:

**Papers:**
Cardstock: white (8" x 6")
Mulberry: claret (4" sq.);
   white (4" x 6")

**Other Materials and Tools:**
Bone folder
Craft scissors
Glue stick
Liquid relief paint: crystal
Pencil
Ruler

# How do I design a card, using layered transparent papers?

The white mulberry paper used on this card is semi-transparent when placed over the darker red hearts, yet you can still see all of the wonderful texture that makes this paper so beautiful. The crystal relief paint accentuates the hearts beautifully, while adding an element of dimension to the card.

## Transparent Paper Card

*Designed by Anneliese Oughton for Anni's Attic*

## Here's how:

1. Using bone folder, fold cardstock in half to form 4" x 6" card. Refer to How do I fold cardstock? on page 18.

2. Draw and cut out two heart shapes approximately 1¾" high from red mulberry paper. Glue hearts, one above the other, onto front of card.

3. Glue white mulberry paper onto front of card.

4. To embellish, create a line of raised dots around heart shapes with crystal liquid relief paint.

**What to Say:**

To the world you may be one person, but to this one person you are the world.

Papers:
Cardstock: white (8" x 6")
Mulberry: claret (4" sq.);
   white (4" x 6")
Watercolor: white (3" sq.)

Other Materials and Tools:
Bone folder
Craft scissors
Glue stick
Liquid relief paint: silver
Paintbrushes: large flat; small
   round
Ruler
Saucer
Watercolor paint: cranberry

# How do I design a card, using torn and layered papers?

Layering torn papers of different colors, patterns, and textures is a wonderfully simple way to give your card a unique look that appears to have taken hours to create, when in reality it took only minutes! Because the edges are torn, you don't have to worry so much about measuring and cutting straight lines. The painted heart design adds a charming touch and is very easy to make.

# Layered Paper Card

*Designed by Anneliese Oughton for Anni's Attic*

## Here's how:

1. Using bone folder, fold cardstock in half to form 4" x 6" card. Refer to How do I fold cardstock? on page 18.

2. Paint watercolor paper, using the following technique:

   a. Using flat paintbrush, thoroughly wet watercolor paper with water, making sweeping strokes from one side to another.

   b. Squeeze some cranberry paint onto saucer and, using round brush, dab a blob of paint onto center of paper. Using flat paintbrush again with water, swirl blob of paint around in small circular motion edging outward. *Note: The water will make the paint bleed. Let dry.*

3. Tear watercolor paper, using the following technique:

   a. Using small paintbrush, wet the tear line on watercolor paper, forming 2" square

   b. Gently tear around line.

4. Using small paintbrush, wet the tear line, forming 3" square on mulberry paper. Tear around line.

5. Glue mulberry square onto front of card. Glue watercolor square onto top of mulberry square.

6. Draw a heart with dots around its outer edge directly onto watercolor square with silver relief paint.

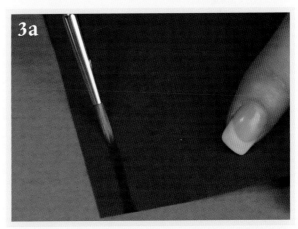

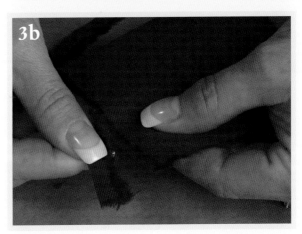

# 5
# technique

## What you need to get started:

Papers:
Cardstock:
   green foil (6" x 4");
   lime green (10" x 7");
   red sparkle (10" x 7")

Other Materials and Tools:
Craft knife
Craft scissors
Cutting mat (or piece of thick
   cardboard)
Glue stick
Masking tape
Metal ruler
Thread: white

A window in a card can hold many surprises. It can hold a greeting, a photograph, or in this case, a twirling Christmas tree. As the card opens, the Christmas tree, suspended by thread, twirls to and fro, delighting the recipient. Remember when you are writing on the inside of your card, to use the space that won't show through the window, unless that is your intent.

# Christmas Tree
# Window Card

*Designed by Jill Dahlberg for Vanessa-Ann Collection*

## Here's how:

1. Using bone folder, fold red-sparkle cardstock in half to form 5" x 7" card. Refer to How do I fold cardstock? on page 18.

2. Draw 2¾" x 4" rectangle on front of card. Open up card so that you do not cut through both sides. Place card on cutting mat. Using metal ruler and craft knife, cut out rectangle, creating a "window" in card.

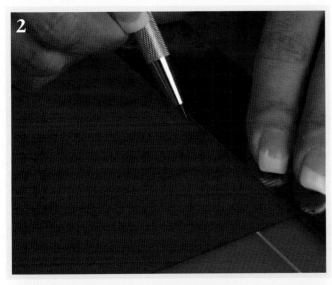

3. Cut lime-green cardstock into two 5" x 7" cards. Using window-card front as a stencil, draw and cut a window in one lime-green card. Make certain windows on both cards are in the exact same position. Set aside.

4. Using Christmas Tree Pattern below, cut two Christmas tree shapes from green foil cardstock.

Christmas Tree Pattern

5. Run 6½" length of thread vertically between the two Christmas trees. *Note: The thread should extend at least 1" beyond the top and bottom of the trees. Glue the trees, wrong sides together.*

6. Center tree in red card's window. Secure thread with tape just above top and bottom of window on inside cover.

7. Glue lime-green window card onto inside cover of red card. *Note: This will hide the tape and give a clean finish.*

8. Glue remaining lime-green card onto inside-right of card.

# 6

## technique

### *What you need to get started:*

Papers:
Cardstock:
   lt. blue polka dot (5¼" x 8½")
Vellum:
   lt. blue patterned (8½" x 11")

Other Materials and Tools:
Computer/printer/paper
Craft scissors
Paper punch
Photograph
Removable tape
Ruler
Sheer ribbon (12")

# How do I design a card, using vellum?

Vellum is a sheer yet sturdy paper that can add an exciting element to cards. No longer only in white, vellum comes in a wide assortment of colors and patterns. The subtle transparency of vellum allows the paper underneath to show through in a soft, muted manner. Vellum also can be run through most computer printers, allowing you to create a personalized greeting. This is a great way to send photographs to family and friends at Christmas.

## Vellum Photo Card

*Designed by Jill Dahlberg for Vanessa-Ann Collection*

### *Here's how:*

*Note: The following instructions are for the card shown on left-hand side of photo at right. Variations also shown.*

1.  On a computer, type in message you want to appear on card. *Note: Your message will be printed on the vellum, but practice on regular printer paper so that you can get the spacing correct. Once it is the way you want it, run the vellum through the printer.*

2.  Trim vellum to approximately ½" smaller on all sides than lt. blue polka-dot cardstock.

3.  Position vellum over cardstock and punch two holes approximately 1" down from top. Thread sheer ribbon through holes and tie into bow.

4.  Trim photograph to fit between bow and greeting. Attach with removable tape. *Note: This will allow the recipient to remove and save the photo, if desired.*

Thinking of you with warm wishes for a
Very Merry Christmas
and a Happy New Year!

The Dahlbergs
Chris, Jill, Bryce, Ben, and Brooke

We wish you a
wonderful holiday season!

Love,
The Dahlberg Family

We wish you Health and Happiness
in the coming year.
Have a Very Happy Holiday!
The Dahlberg Family
Chris, Jill, Bryce, Ben & Brooke

# 7
## technique

### *What you need to get started:*

Papers:
Cardstock:
   metallic gold (5¼" x 7");
   pink (scraps); red (scraps);
   white (10" x 7")

Other Materials and Tools:
Adhesive-foam dots
Bone folder
Fine-tipped marker:
   metallic gold
Glue stick
Heart paper punch
Ruler
Thin cord: metallic gold (24")

# How do I design a card, using punch art?

Whatever shape you can think of, there is probably a paper punch available to help when you want to cut more than one of the same shape. Some craft and scrapbook stores even allow you to use their punches free of charge when you buy your paper from them. Of course, you can trace your desired motifs and cut them out individually, but paper punches certainly make a project less tedious.

# Punched Hearts Card

*Designed by Jill Dahlberg for Vanessa-Ann Collection*

## Here's how:

1. Using bone folder, fold white cardstock in half to form approximately 5" x 7" card, not quite bringing edges together, so that there is ¼" gap on right-hand side. Refer to How do I fold cardstock? on page 18.

2. Center and glue metallic-gold cardstock onto inside-right of card. *Note: When the card is closed, this will create a nice gold edge.*

3. Punch out four heart shapes from pink cardstock and five heart shapes from red cardstock.

4. Using metallic-gold marker, draw checks, dots, or squiggles onto each heart.

5. Mount hearts onto front of card with adhesive-foam dots. Tie gold cord around fold of card.

## Punch-art Variation:

*Punch-art shapes can be found to fit almost any theme. Have fun creating your own unique announcements for new babies or shower invitations for new moms or lingerie parties for the bride-to-be. Key your paper colors to the honored guest's taste, gender, and the party theme.*

# How do I design a card, using a glass stone?

## What you need to get started:

Papers:
Cardstock:
    textured white (7" x 5");
    white (2¾" x 2½")

Other Materials and Tools:
Bone folder
Craft glue: clear-drying
Craft scissors
Double-stick tape
Fine-tipped marker: black
Glass flat-backed stone
Pencil
Watercolor markers: desired
    palette

Using glass stones over artwork gives the illusion of the artwork actually being inside of the stone. Make certain to choose stones that are flat-backed so that they can be attached securely to the card. Create a simple design such as these flowers; or experiment using stickers, motifs, patterned paper, photographs, or printed type under the stone.

## Glass Stone Card

*Designed by Jill Dahlberg for Vanessa-Ann Collection*

### Here's how:

1. Using bone folder, fold textured cardstock in half to form 5" x 3½" card. Refer to How do I fold cardstock? on page 18.

2. Place glass stone in center of white cardstock and trace around shape with pencil. Remove stone and sketch the design you want to have show through. Color design with markers, and outline in black. Glue stone over top of design.

3. Write "Thanks!" or desired message below stone, and mount onto front of textured card with double-stick tape.

# How do I design a card, using beads and charms as embellishments?

There are so many different beads and charms on the market that you will have no problem finding just the right embellishments for your card. In the case of this "congratulations" card for a new baby girl, the sterling silver pacifier charm can be removed and used later on a bracelet or necklace.

## Beads & Charms Baby Card

*Designed by Jill Dahlberg for Vanessa-Ann Collection*

### Here's how:

1. Using the bone folder, fold cardstock in half to form 5" square card. Refer to How do I fold cardstock? on page 18.

2. Using fine-tipped marker, print "congratulations" on lower half of card in very small letters.

3. Using glue pen, place dots of glue on beads and adhere as desired.

4. Tie ribbon to pacifier charm, and trim ends. Using craft glue, adhere pacifier and star charms onto card.

## What you need to get started:

Papers:
Cardstock: white (10" x 5")

Other Materials and Tools:
Bone folder
Craft glue
Craft scissors
Fine-tipped marker, black
Glue pen
Satin ribbon: ⅟₁₆"-wide, pink (3")
Seed beads: pink; white
Silver charms: pacifier; star

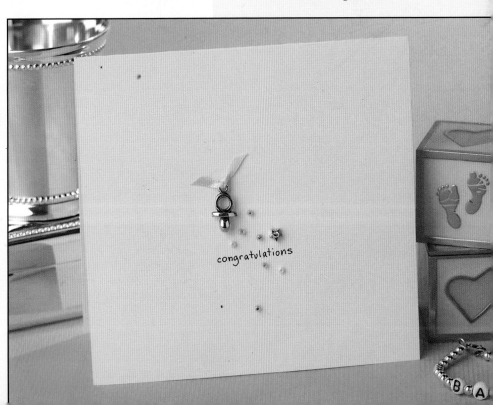

# 10
## technique

### What you need to get started:

**Papers:**
Cardstock: red (3" x 4");
   white textured (8" x 6");
   yellow (2" x 3")

**Other Materials and Tools:**
Beading needle: sharp
Beading thread: clear
Bone folder
Craft glue
Craft scissors
Fine-tipped marker: black
Ladybug button
Ruler
Seed beads: black (6); red (12)

## How do I sew objects onto a card?

Sewing beads onto your card, rather than gluing them, gives your designs "movable" dimension. It also helps to keep the beads attached. Sewing through paper isn't difficult if you make certain to use a very sharp needle with a small eye. This will slide through the paper easily, and will leave only a small hole. For added security, you could place tape over the knots on the back so that they won't come up through the holes.

# Beaded Ladybug Birthday Card

*Designed by Joyleene Abrey for Snowflake Cards*

## Here's how:

1. Using bone folder, fold white cardstock in half to form 4" x 6" card. Refer to How do I fold cardstock? on page 18.

2. Thread needle and knot ends. Starting in upper-left corner of yellow paper, bring needle up through the back. Add three beads onto needle—red, black, red. Push needle back down through paper and come up again ¼" away from first set of beads. Repeat beading sequence until there are three sets of beads along top edge.

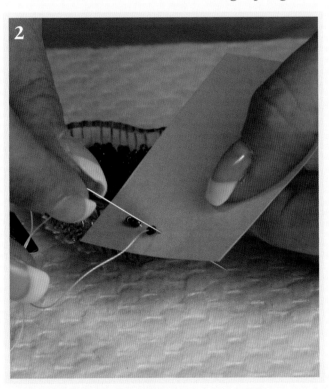

3. Measure 1½" down from this row of beads, and repeat directly underneath. Knot thread securely on the back and cut off.

4. Glue ladybug button between bead rows. *Note: If your button has a shank, trim it off with wire cutters so that it lies flat, or you can sew the button on. Gently tear around edges. Refer to Technique 4, Step 3a–b on page 27.*

5. Mount artwork onto red paper. Gently tear around edges, leaving a ¼" border.

6. Mount layered artwork onto front of card.

7. Using the fine-tipped marker, write "Happy Birthday" under artwork.

## Sewing Variation:

*Fold under the top and side edges of a beaded practice swatch. Pull threads to fringe the bottom edge and sew swatch to card.*

# How do I design a card, using paper-embossing?

Paper embossing is a simple technique that gives your cards a very professional look. There is a large variety in embossing templates on the market, with styles ranging from country cute to simple elegance. Paper made especially for embossing is patterned or colored on one side only; however, you also could use heavy white paper for the formal white-on-white effect used on wedding announcements. If you do not have a light-box, a well-lit window will also work.

## What you need to get started:

**Papers:**
Embossing papers: blue
   small polka dot; green small
   polka dot; lavender medium
   polka dot; lavender plaid;
   pink small polka dot
   (1 sheet each)

**Other Materials and Tools:**
Bone folder
Craft scissors
Double-stick tape
Embossing stylus
Embossing templates: flower;
   house with heart
Glue stick
Light-box
Ruler
Waxed paper (optional)

## Embossed Paper House Card

*Designed by Lorilyn Tenney*

### Here's how:

1.  Cut lavender plaid paper to measure 8½" x 5½". Using bone folder, fold in half to form 4¼" x 5½" card. Refer to How do I fold cardstock? on page 18.

2.  Secure house template onto light-box with small strip of double-stick tape. *Note: Keep tape along the edge of template, if possible, to avoid letting the tape show through large open areas of the template.*

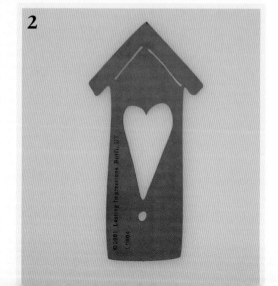

2

Continued on page 40.

What to Say:

May all your **days** be filled with **sunshine**,
all your **nights** with **romance**,
and the **time** in between with **love.**

Continued from page 38.

3. Place blue polka-dot paper over template, white side facing you. *Note: It is easier to see through the paper when the room is dark or very dimly lit and only the light-box is illuminated.*

4. Using fingers, gently rub over area of paper to be embossed. *Note: This creates a slightly slick surface for the stylus to move over.*

5. Paper emboss, using the following technique:

   a. Hold paper firmly down on top of template and use large-balled end of stylus to gently trace around outer edge of house. *Notes: Using a very light touch and going over the same section several times will emboss without tearing through the paper.*

   *Do not move the paper until the design has been embossed.*

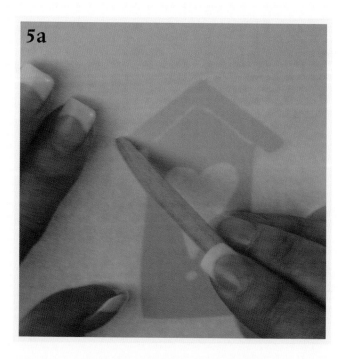

b. Use smaller end of stylus to trace "roof" details of house.

c. Remove lavender paper from light-box.

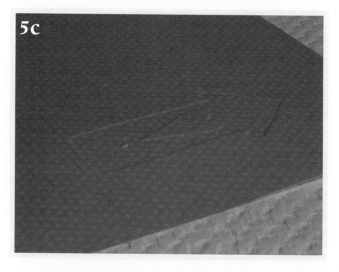

d. Place pink polka-dot paper over template, white side up. Emboss heart only. Remove paper and house template from light-box.

e. Secure flower template onto light-box with double-stick tape, as in Step 2 on page 38. Place pink polka-dot paper over template and emboss flower only. Remove pink paper from light-box.

f. Place green polka-dot paper over template. Emboss leaves only.

6. Using scissors, carefully trim around house, leaving ⅛" border. Trim around heart, flower, and leaves. *Note: When trimming leaves, keep them attached by a small strip of paper between them to make for easier handling when gluing and positioning them.*

7. Apply light layer of glue to back of heart and position onto house. Apply glue along front of strip connecting leaves and position flower between them. Apply glue to back of flower and leaves and position onto house underneath the heart.

8. Glue house onto lavender polka-dot paper, leaving approximately 1" space around house. Gently tear around edges to form a rectangular shape around house.

9. Glue house artwork onto front of card.

## Embossed Paper Variations:

*You can tell by looking at the cards below, that simply changing your color scheme can give your cards a whole new look and feel. The wings of the dragonflies are made from vellum and give extra dimension to the card's embossing. This easy Christmas card is one that everyone in the family can help create. One person can do the embossing, another can cut out the shapes, and another can position the shapes on the cards. Your cards will have the homemade feel, but the embossing will give them that polished store-bought look.*

## What you need to get started:

**Papers:**
Cardstock: cream (3" x 5");
  lt. green (6½" x 5½");
  periwinkle (3" x 5")

**Other Materials and Tools:**
Bone folder
Brass brad (¼")
Craft scissors
Dauber Duos ™:
  amethyst/raspberry;
  pink/apricot;
  violet/heliotrope
Glitter glue
Glue stick
Hole punch
Organza ribbon: pink (8")
Rubber stamps: birthday
  birdie; candle cake
Watercolor paints, markers, or colored pencils

# How do I design a card, using rubber stamps?

Because of the thousands of rubber stamps there are to choose from, almost anyone can become an artist. Simply stamp the image onto paper and "color between the lines" with watercolor paints, markers, or even crayons.

## Rubber-stamped Birthday Tag

*Designed by Jennifer Lynch for Personal Stamp Exchange*

### Here's how:

1. Stamp, using the candle cake stamp and following technique:

   a. Ink stamp with the Dauber Duos, placing different colors randomly over stamp. *Note: The part of the rubber stamp that makes the impression is the raised part. The recessed part of the image does not print and, therefore, should not be colored.*

Continued on page 44.

How old would you be
if you didn't know how old you were?

12    8    29   21        52   40   45
  35          16

Continued from page 42.

b. Stamp image onto cream cardstock by placing stamp, rubber-die side down. Without rocking or twisting the stamp, apply a little pressure.

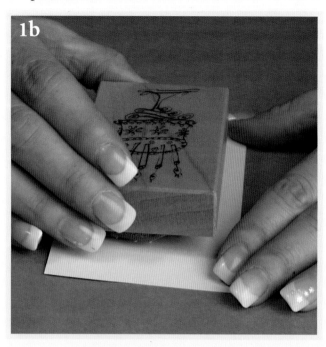

c. Lift stamp straight up and off cardstock.

2. Repeat Step 1a–c on page 42 and at left with birthday birdie stamp, violet dauber, and periwinkle cardstock.

3. Color images, using one of the following methods:

**Colored Pencils:**
a. If using colored pencils, use the pencil marks to add texture to the stamped image. *Note: Crosshatching or coloring in one direction produces interesting results, as does coloring an area with two coordinating colors.*

**Markers:**
a. If using markers, proceed in order from lightest color first to darkest color last. *Note: That way, you are less likely to drag darker colors into lighter colors.*

**Watercolor paints:**
a. If using watercolor paints, fully load wet paintbrush, then make tiny circles in desired color. *Note: Test watercolor paints on scrap paper to see if the color is too strong or too weak. If necessary, add more water or more paint to adjust the effect.*

4. Using Tag Pattern at right, cut images into a tag shape. *Note: Make certain that birthday birdie image is positioned on the lower-right corner of tag.*

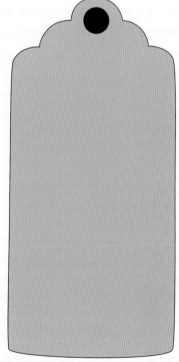

Tag Pattern

5.  Punch a hole in top of both tags. Thread ribbon through holes and tie into bow.

6.  Using bone folder, fold green cardstock in half to form 3¼" x 5½" card. Refer to How do I fold cardstock? on page 18. Trim top corners.

7.  Using glue stick, adhere tags onto card. Punch a hole at top and insert brad.

8.  Embellish design with glitter glue, as desired.

**How to Thread a Gift Tag Ribbon** (as shown above)**:**

1.  Fold ribbon in half.

2.  Insert folded end of ribbon through punched hole and pull through approximately 2".

3.  Using fingers, open up folded end to form a loop.

4.  Thread loose ends through the loop.

5.  Pull loose ends gently so that loop tightens around card.

## What you need to get started:

**Papers:**
Cardstock: white (8" x 6")
Mulberry: lt. blue (4" sq.);
   white (2" sq.)
Parchment: translucent (3" sq.)

**Other Materials and Tools:**
Baby feet rubber stamp
Bone folder
Craft scissors
Embossing heat tool
Embossing powder: metallic
   silver
Glue stick
Pigment ink embossing pad

# How do I design a card, using heat-embossing?

Embossing is a great way to give a card dimension and add that little extra touch of sophistication. There are thousands of stamp designs available, as well as a large, colorful variety of embossing powders and inks. Make certain to use a pigment ink, which is slow drying. This is important because you want your image to stay as wet as possible in order for the embossing powder to stick and give you a clear design.

# Embossed Baby Feet Card

*Designed by Anneliese for Anni's Attic*

## Here's how:

1. Using bone folder, fold cardstock in half to form 4" x 6" card. Refer to How do I fold cardstock? on page 18.

2. Press rubber stamp onto embossing pad.

3. Stamp onto parchment paper. Refer to Technique 12, Step 1a–c on pages 42–44.

4. Heat-emboss with metallic silver powder, using the following technique:

   a. While ink is still wet, sprinkle silver embossing powder over image until covered completely. Shake off excess powder. *Note: If you shake the powder onto a clean piece of paper, you can pour it back into the container to reuse.*

   b. Using heat tool, gently blow hot air over image at a distance of approximately 4" until powder melts into a smooth image. *Note: Be careful not to overheat the image or the embossing powder will bubble and the image will not be clear.* Let image cool.

5. Cut parchment into rectangular shape around embossed image.

6. Tear a slightly larger rectangle from white mulberry paper. Refer to Technique 4, Step 3a–b on page 27. Glue image in place.

7. Tear a third and larger rectangle from lt. blue mulberry paper. Mount image onto lt. blue, and glue entire piece onto front of card.

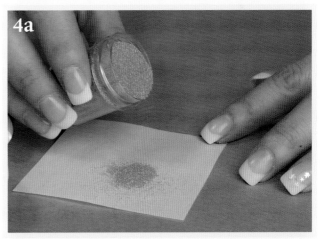

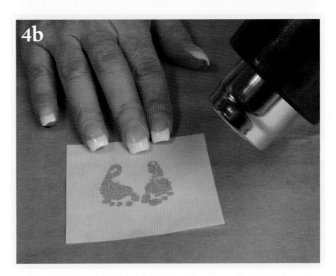

# 14
## technique

### *What you need to get started:*

**Papers:**
Cardstock: gray (6" x 3¾");
  scraps; tan (5¾" x 3½");
  white (8 " x 6 ¼")

**Other Materials and Tools:**
Adhesive-foam dots
Bone folder
Camp theme stickers
Craft knife
Double-stick tape
Photograph (optional)

# How do I design a card, using stickers?

Stickers are no longer just single images. Today, there are entire scenes available, such as this delightful Camping Out scene from Personal Stamp Exchange. Choose stickers that have removable areas, allowing you to place a photograph in that space. Additionally, the use of adhesive-foam dots gives more dimension to your card.

## Happy Camper Sticker Card

*Designed by Stephanie Scheetz for Personal Stamp Exchange*

### *Here's how:*

1. Using bone folder, fold white cardstock in half to form 6¼" x 4" card. Refer to How do I fold cardstock? on page 18.

2. Arrange stickers onto tan paper as desired. *Note: The trailer sticker used in this project has a door that can be removed, allowing you to tape a photograph behind the sticker.*

3. Adhere one or two sticker motifs onto cardstock scrap, and cut around shapes.

4. Position on scene, using adhesive-foam dots to raise them off the card.

5. Mount scene onto gray paper with double-stick tape. Mount again onto front of card.

# How do I design a card, using the tea bag folding technique?

## What you need to get started:

**Papers:**
Cardstock: green (2" sq.),
  red (3" sq.)
Embossed note card:
  green (5½" x 4¼")
Tea bag paper: Christmas
  poinsettia design (for eight
  2" sq.)

**Other Materials and Tools:**
Craft knife
Craft scissors
Cutting mat (or heavy
  cardboard)
Decorative corner punch
Double-stick tape
Glue pen
Glue stick
Metal ruler

Tea bag folding is a paper art form that originated from folding the paper envelopes in which tea bags are packaged. Tea bag paper is a very thin, lightweight paper that has a printed pattern on one side and is plain or colored on the other side. Each sheet contains small squares of the same design. These squares must be cut out individually before you begin folding. In lieu of tea bag paper, you could use any lightweight paper that has a pattern only on one side.

## Tea Bag Folded Flower Card

*Designed by Laura Lees for L. Paper Designs*

## Here's how:

1.  Place tea bag paper onto cutting mat. Using a metal ruler and craft knife for a straight edge, cut out eight 2" design squares.

2.  Fold tea bag paper to create a flower, using the following technique. *Note: You may want to practice on one square by labeling corners A, B, C, and D as shown.*

    a.  With right sides together, fold D to A, forming a triangle. Open flat.  **a**

    b.  With right sides together, fold C to B, forming a triangle. Open flat.  **b**

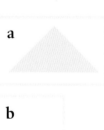

Continued on page 52.

**What to Say:**

A single flower can fill a room with sunshine.
A single act of kindness can fill a heart with joy.

Continued from page 50.

c. With wrong side up, fold A/B to C/D. Open flat.

**c**

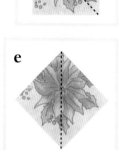

**d**

d. With wrong side up, fold B/D to A/C.

e. Pick up rectangle, with open edge up. Hold lower corners and push toward center, forming four triangles. Bring two triangles to each side to form a square. *Note: At this point, choose which pattern you want to feature and make all eight pieces with the same design showing. To change the pattern, rotate the triangles around until you have chosen another pattern.*

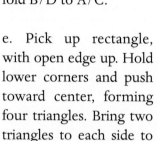

**e**

f. Lay one piece down on table with open edge at top. Pick up one triangle from left side and fold over to right side.

g. Bring point of same triangle back to center and crease.

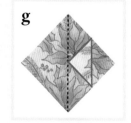

**g**

h. Fold same piece back to left side.

i. Pick up triangle from right side and fold over to left side.

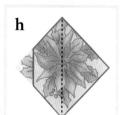

**h**

j. Bring point of same triangle back to center and crease.

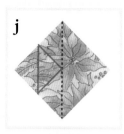

**j**

k. Fold same piece back to right side.

l. Repeat with remaining pieces.

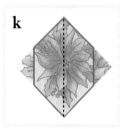

**k**

m. To assemble a flower, pick up one piece with folded edges at bottom. Using glue pen, apply a thin line of glue along left long folded crease. With second piece held in the same manner, slide glued edge between the two layers of second piece, overlapping design at center and aligning points at bottom edge.

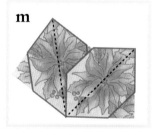

**m**

n. Continue adding pieces in the same manner from right side.

o. For the remaining piece, insert as usual, but bring the glued edge forward and between layers to complete the circle. *Note: You will have a small hole in the center.*

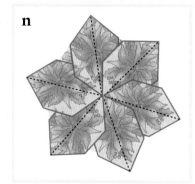

**n**

3.  Trim corners of red cardstock with decorative corner punch. Mount onto front of green note card with double-stick tape.

4.  Mount green cardstock diagonally onto center of red square with double-stick tape.

5.  Adhere flower onto front of card with glue stick.

Tea bag paper is usually premarked with hatch marks that run vertically and horizontally. It comes in a variety of colors and patterns.

## What you need to get started:

**Papers:**
Cardstock: red (6¼" x 13¼");
 dk. green (scrap);
 lt. green (8½" x 11");
 white (8½" x 11")
Patterned: green/white
 polka dot (8½" x 11");
 red/white (scrap)

**Other Materials and Tools:**
Adhesive-foam dots
Computer/printer
Craft scissors
Embroidery flosses: green; red
Fine-tipped marker: black
Glue stick
Ruler
Stickers: hearts, red; tag, gold
Tracing paper

# How do I create a card, using accordion pleats?

Accordion cards involve the folding of paper into accordion pleats. The pleats can vary in number and size and can be presented horizontally or vertically. The pleats fold up fairly flat, but will spread when opened to reveal several layers of design in a card. In this accordion-folded card, the hands appear to be applauding when the card sits open. It can be displayed with the covers lying flat or with the covers sitting up.

# Accordion Card

*Designed by Sandi Genovese for Ellison®*

## *Here's how:*

1. Using bone folder, fold cardstock for front and back cover 4⅛" from each end. Refer to How do I fold cardstock? on page 18.

2. Using bone folder, fold interior pleats ⅛" each.

3. Using Hand Pattern at right, trace 13 hands onto tracing paper, then cut out patterns. Transfer patterns onto white cardstock. Cut out designs.

4. Cut nine 1" x ½" pieces and four 1" squares from green/white polka-dot paper for cuffs. Cut one 1" x ½" piece from red/white paper.

5. Using glue stick, adhere a cuff onto each wrist. Adhere 12 hands onto pleats, placing the hands with 1" square cuffs in the center row of the pleats. *Note: This allows the hands to sit taller in order to move freely and not catch on the outside hands.* Adhere heart stickers onto hands as desired. Tie a bow on one finger with green embroidery floss.

6. Print messages on lt. green cardstock. Cut to desired size. Center and adhere messages onto dk. green cardstock. Cut dk. green cardstock, leaving ¼" border all around. Adhere onto inside-front and inside-back of card.

7. Cut 2" x 3¼" piece from lt. green cardstock. Cut 2½" x 3¾" from dk. green cardstock. Center and adhere lt. green cardstock onto dk. green cardstock. Using glue stick, adhere mat onto front of card.

8. Using fine-tipped marker, write message on gold tag sticker.

9. Tie tag to finger of remaining hand with red embroidery floss. Adhere sticker to secure.

10. Using adhesive-foam dots, adhere remaining hand onto green mat on front of card.

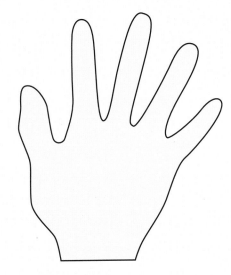

Hand Pattern

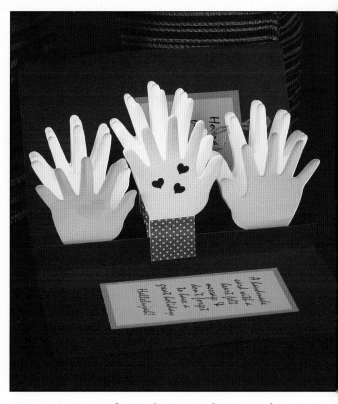

*Designer's Note: If you do not wish to use the patterns provided, die-cuts are an option. Die-cuts are precut shapes of paper or lightweight cardstock. Die-cuts are available at all craft, stationery, and scrapbook stores. Die-cuts are especially convenient when making repetitive patterns.*

55

## What you need to get started:

Papers:
Cardstock: blue (8 sheets);
  gold (2 sheets);
  lt. gold (scrap);
  red (2 sheets);
  white (1 sheet)

Other Materials and Tools:
Adhesive-foam dots
Border sticker (10")
Craft scissors
Double-stick tape
Glue stick
Tracing paper

# How do I create a multidimensional card?

Multidimensional cards are great for any occasion or special event. Change the colors and the message and this "Thanks" card can be quickly converted to any holiday or special event. The size of the squares will dictate the ultimate size of the card.

# Multidimensional Card

*Designed by Sandi Genovese for Ellison*®

## Here's how:

1. Cut seven 8" squares and one 2½" square from blue cardstock. Cut seven 2½" squares and two 4½" squares from red cardstock. Cut eight 1½" squares from gold cardstock. Cut one 1½" square from lt. gold cardstock.

2. Using Letter Patterns at right, trace patterns onto tracing paper, then cut out patterns. Transfer patterns onto white cardstock. Cut out letters. Using Heart Pattern on page 58, trace pattern onto tracing paper, then cut out pattern. Transfer pattern onto red cardstock. Cut out design.

3. Using bone folder to crease folded lines, mountain-fold each 8" blue square in half by length. Open and mountain-fold in half in by width. Open and valley-fold in half on the diagonal. Refer to How do I fold cardstock? on page 18.

4. Using double-stick tape, adhere folded squares in a long strip, overlapping one-fourth of each square.

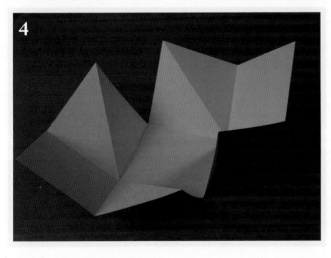

Letter Patterns

5. Using glue stick, center and adhere one gold square at a 90° angle onto one red square. Repeat six times. Center and adhere one letter onto each square.

6. Decorate each inside square with a matted letter spelling out "Thanks."

7. Center and adhere lt. gold square onto remaining gold square. Center and adhere gold square onto 2½" blue square. Center and adhere onto one 4½" red square.

8. Adhere red squares onto top and bottom folded square, with decorative square on top.

9. Cut 10" x ¾" piece from gold cardstock. Wrap around card. Adhere strip ends together, creating band for card.

10. Adhere long sticker around band.

11. Adhere heart onto center front of band with adhesive foam dot.

Heart Pattern

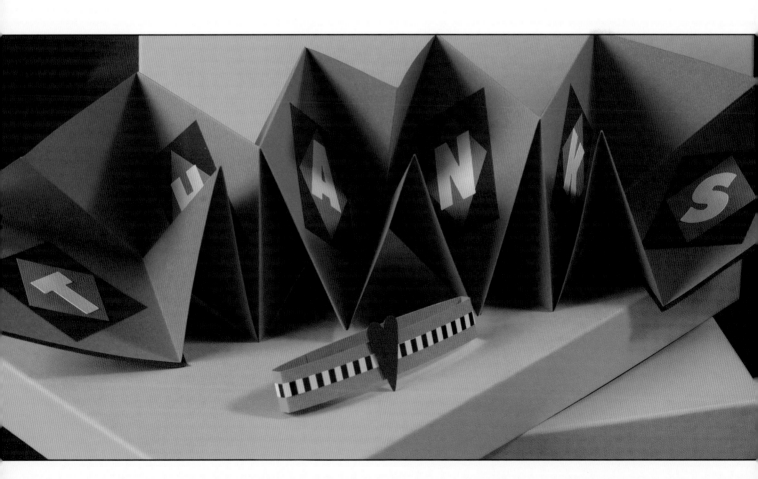

58

# How do I create a pop-up card?

Pop-up tabs that are arranged at even intervals are the perfect place to feature one shape that is repeated. When attaching shapes to pop-up tabs, close card and make certain the shapes are not peeking out. If they are exposed, simply make the card cover wider/longer to keep the shapes concealed until the card is opened and they pop-up.

## What you need to get started:

Papers:
Cardstock: blue (1 sheet); gold (1 sheet); red (1 sheet); white (6½" x 10½")

Other Materials and Tools:
Adhesive-foam dots
Bone folder
Computer/printer
Craft scissors
Die-cuts: palm tree (6); shirt; sun (2); surfboard (patterns have been provided, if you cannot find appropriate die-cuts)
Double-stick tape
Fine-tipped marker: silver
Glue stick
Metal ruler
Pencil
Photocopy machine
Pigment ink stamp pad
Stickers: water
Tracing paper
Wave pattern rubber stamp

# Pop-up Card

*Designed by Sandi Genovese for Ellison®*

## Here's how:

1. Using bone folder, fold white cardstock to form 6½" x 5¼" card cover. Refer to How do I fold cardstock? on page 18.

2. Enlarge Pop-up Card Pattern on page 61 200%. Trace pattern onto tracing paper, then cut out pattern. Transfer pattern onto blue cardstock. Cut out design, creasing on dotted lines and cutting on solid lines. Using bone folder, fold pop-up card as indicated. *Note: If using provided patterns instead of die-cuts, trace patterns onto tracing paper. Cut out patterns. Transfer patterns onto desired cardstock. Cut out designs.*

3. Using double-stick tape, adhere card to inside of card cover. Adhere surfboard to front tab and palm trees on remaining tabs.

4. Print party information on gold cardstock. Center and glue onto red cardstock. Cut around red cardstock, leaving ⅛" border all around. Glue red cardstock to bottom of card. Decorate with water stickers as desired.

5. Layer and glue suns together. Adhere suns to top of card with adhesive-foam dot.

6. Cut 5¾" x 4¾" piece from red cardstock. Using glue stick, adhere to card cover. Cut 4½" x 2½" piece from blue cardstock.

9. Using wave pattern rubber stamp, stamp blue piece of cardstock. Refer to Technique 12, Step 1a–c on pages 42–44. Glue to front of card as desired.

10. Decorate shirt as desired. Adhere to front of card cover with adhesive-foam dot.

11. Using the fine-tipped marker, write desired message.

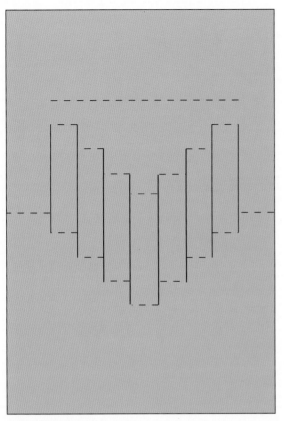

Pop-up Card Pattern

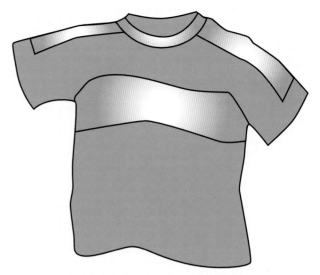

Shirt Pattern

Sun Pattern

Palm Tree Pattern

Surfboard Pattern

# 19
## technique

### What you need to get started:

Papers:
Cardstock: ivory (10⅝" x 8")
Matching envelope (8½" x 5½")
 (optional)

Other Materials and Tools:
Bone folder
Calligraphy pen: black
Ink pads (optional)
Leaf stamp (optional)
Metal ruler
Paper punch
Photocopy machine (optional)
Ribbon: 1"-wide, metallic (28")
Rosebud stamp (optional)
Watercolor paintbrush
Watercolor paints: transparent

# How do I design a card, using hand-painting or artwork?

When someone skilled with a calligraphy pen creates a handwritten card or invitation, it is exceptionally elegant. To add extra beauty and personality to such a card, embellish it with a flourish of hand-painted flower-bud stems. With the many foliage and floral stamps available today, even those who are not experienced artists can produce the lovely appearance of transparent watercolor. Tie the card closed with an exquisite gauzy ribbon.

# Hand-painted Invitation

*Designed by Sara Toliver for Vanessa-Ann Collection*

## Here's how:

1. Using calligraphy pen, create one master card on ivory cardstock.

2. Photocopy master card onto as many cards as desired.

3. Using watercolor paintbrush and paints, embellish card with bud stem. Let dry.

4. Using bone folder, fold card with sides opening at center and words on the inside. Refer to How do I fold cardstock? on page 18.

5. Using hole punch, punch holes in center edge of each flap.

6. Place open card face down. Place ribbon horizontally across center of card. Thread ribbon ends from inside of card. Pull ends taut.

7. Turn card over, close, and tie ribbon ends in a loose bow with trailing ends. Present as is or tuck into a roomy matching envelope.

## Hand-painted and Artwork Variation:

*The cards below were created by adhering artwork onto the folded cardstock. The artwork can be your original or items you cut from wrapping paper, junk mail, magazines, or photographs. Enhance "found" art with colored pencils, paints, or crayons. Stickers and stamps can also be employed.*

## What you need to get started:

Papers:
Cardstock:
   textured, craft (10" x 5")

Other Materials and Tools:
Bone folder
Pressed flowers
Spray adhesive
Waxed paper

# How do I design a card, using pressed flowers?

Pressed flowers and leaves give your cards a natural, elegant look. They come prepackaged in most craft stores so that you don't have to press them yourself. However, if you have a garden full of beautiful blooms, you may want to learn more about the craft. Remember that pressed flowers are extremely delicate, so take care when handling. Spray adhesive is your best choice when adhering the flowers to your card. For added protection, you may want to lightly brush a small amount of découpage over the flowers once they are in position, helping to seal the edges.

# Pressed Flower Card

*Designed by Jo Packham for Vanessa-Ann Collection*

## Here's how:

1. Using bone folder, fold cardstock in half to form 5" square card. Refer to How do I fold cardstock? on page 18.

2. Position flowers onto front of card as desired. Gently lift flowers and apply spray adhesive to back side. Reposition onto front of card.

3. Place a piece of waxed paper over flowers and gently press to set flowers in place.

## Pressed Flower Variation:

*The card below was designed by LuAnn Vermillion of Wildflowers by LuAnn. Because Queen Anne's Lace is so fragile, these flowers are protected by a piece of wide, clear tape. This is a good option when you know your card is going to be handled often.*

# 21

## technique

### What you need to get started:

**Papers:**
Cardstock: lavender (8½" x 5½");
    yellow (5" x 3")
Patterned:
lavender checked (4¼" x 1¼")
Vellum (scrap)

**Other Materials and Tools:**
Bone folder
Clear tape
Craft glue
Craft scissors
Cutting mat (or something to
    protect work surface)
Eyelets
Eyelet tools (punch and setter)
Fine-tipped marker: black
Flower punch
Hammer
Paintbrush
Yarns and threads (scraps)

## How do I use eyelets in my card design?

If you want to add a little something extra to your cards, try adding eyelets. They can be used to add dimension, lace ribbons together, or as a hole for attaching tags. Eyelets come in all different shapes, sizes, and colors. If a sturdier eyelet is required—to hold several items together on heavier paper or cardboard—there are heavy-duty eyelets available. Eyelets are also a nice touch when adding fabric scraps to your cards.

# Eyelet Flower Card

*Designed by Jill Dahlberg for Vanessa-Ann Collection*

## Here's how:

1.  Using bone folder, fold lavender cardstock in half to form 5½" x 4¼" card. Refer to How do I fold cardstock? on page 18.

2.  Cut yellow cardstock to 4½" x 1½". Adhere lavender-checked paper to front of yellow strip.

3.  Wrap strip lengthwise with various yarns and threads and secure to back with tape.

4.  Punch three flower shapes from remaining piece of yellow cardstock.

5.  Place cutting mat onto work surface. Position eyelet punch tool over center of flower, and lightly tap with hammer to punch hole.

6.  Attach eyelets, using the following technique:

    a.  Insert eyelet into hole. Position setting tool over eyelet.

    b.  Using hammer, tap to set.

7.  Glue flowers onto front of strip.

8.  Cut 2" square from vellum. Gently tear along bottom edge. Refer to Technique 4, Step 3a–b on page 27.

9.  Using the fine-tipped marker, write desired sentiment onto vellum.

10. Adhere vellum onto front of card. Position and adhere decorated strip onto front of card, overlapping top edge of vellum.

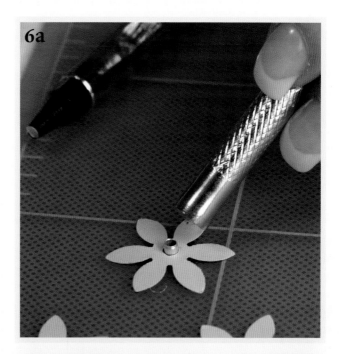

6a

6b

# Section 3: beyond the basics

## What you need to get started:

Papers:
Cardstock: cream (5¼" x 3¼");
   white (3" x 2") (8½" x 5½")
Vellum: lt. blue (4" sq.);
   lt. green (4" sq.);
   lt. pink (4" sq.)

Other Materials and Tools:
Archival pigment ink pads:
   pink; purple; turquoise
Bone folder
Craft scissors
Double-stick tape
Glue stick
Rubber stamps: birthday
   birdies; party hats
Thin gold cord (20")

# How do I design a card with envelope pockets?

This card combines rubber stamping with the use of vellum and paper folding. These fun little pockets can contain additional messages, photographs, coupons, or even small gifts. This same technique can be used to make a larger pocket for a gift certificate, theater tickets, or cash.

# Envelope Pocket Party Invitation

*Designed by Stephanie Scheetz for Personal Stamp Exchange*

## Here's how:

1. Ink birthday birdie stamps in desired colors and randomly stamp the images on cream cardstock. Refer to Technique 12, Step 1a–c on pages 42–44.

2. Cut 3" x 2" white cardstock into thirds (1" x 2"). On each third, stamp a party hat in desired color.

3. Fold each vellum square corner to corner, and cut in half.

4. Place one party hat card in the center of a vellum triangle. Wrap vellum around piece on sides and bottom to form an envelope.

5. Repeat with other pieces of vellum.

6. Mount envelopes onto stamped cardstock with double-stick tape.

7. Using bone folder, fold white cardstock in half to form a 5½" x 4¼" card. Refer to How do I fold cardstock? on page 18.

8. Mount artwork onto front of card with double-stick tape.

9. Tie gold cord around fold of card.

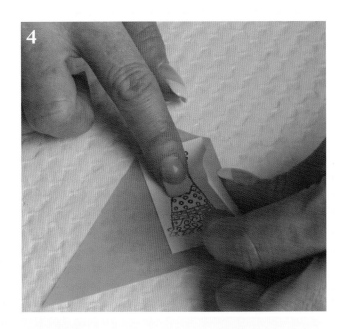

# How do I design a card, using woven papers?

## *What you need to get started:*

**Papers:**
Cardstock:
  metallic gold (2½" x 4");
  sage green (8½" x 5½");
  white (2½" x 4")
Colored: lt. green (5¼" x 4")
Vellum: lilac (3" x 3½");
  lt. pink (4" sq.)

**Other Materials and Tools:**
Adhesive-foam dots
Bone folder
Craft knife
Craft scissors
Double-stick tape
Flower stickers: clear-backed
  hydrangeas; violets
Glue stick
Metal ruler
Photo corners: gold (4)

Weaving strips of paper together is a simple way to create a sophisticated look for your cards. In this project, the designer has used vellum for weaving. A sticker was placed on one of the pieces of vellum so that when they were woven together, part of the design was muted, creating a beautiful screen effect.

# Woven Paper Card

*Designed by Stephanie Scheetz for Personal Stamp Exchange*

## Here's how:

1. Using bone folder, fold sage-green cardstock in half to form 4¼" x 5½" card. Refer to How do I fold cardstock? on page 18.

2. Adhere violet stickers onto white cardstock. Using metal ruler and craft knife, trim cardstock to 2" x 3½" rectangle.

3. Mount violet card onto metallic-gold cardstock. Trim, leaving ⅛" border. Set aside.

4. Adhere hydrangea sticker onto pink vellum. Trim to 3½" x 3".

5. Weave papers together using the following technique:

   a. Cut pink vellum into ⅜" strips. Place pink strips horizontally.

   b. Cut lilac vellum into ⅜" strips.

   c. Weave purple vellum strips vertically into pink vellum strips. Using glue stick, adhere strips in place.

6. Mount woven strips onto pale green paper at an angle with double-stick tape. Attach photo corners.

7. Mount onto card front with double-stick tape.

8. Mount violet card onto front of card with adhesive-foam dots.

*Designer's Note: The stickers used in this design were Blue Hydrangeas and Violets by Personal Stamp Exchange. Be certain to choose stickers that have a clear background. This allows you to place them on any color of paper, and the paper will show through the sticker.*

# How do I combine the tea bag folding technique with a window card?

## What you need to get started:

**Papers:**
Cardstock: burgundy
(10½" x 5½");
green (4" square)
Tea bag paper: Christmas
berry and leaf design (for
eighteen 2" squares)

**Other Materials and Tools:**
Circle cutter
Craft knife
Craft scissors
Cutting mat (or heavy
cardboard)
Glue pen
Glue stick
Metal ruler

This card features another tea bag folding technique—the Sunburst design. This design looks very complicated, but is actually quite easy. The individual pieces form a wreath that is placed over a "window" on the card. The kaleidoscope-like design this creates on the outside is equally delightful on the inside.

# Sunburst Folded Flower Card

*Designed by Laura Lees for L. Paper Designs*

## Here's how:

1. Place tea bag paper onto cutting mat. Using metal ruler and craft knife for straight edges, cut out eighteen 2" design squares.

2. Fold the tea bag paper to create a starburst, using the following technique. *Note: You may want to practice on one square by labeling corners A, B, C, and D as shown.*

| A | B |
|---|---|
| C | D |

a. With right side up, fold C/D to A/B and crease. Open flat.

b. Turn clockwise one-half turn. Fold B/D to A/C and crease. Open flat.

c. With wrong side up, bring A to D, forming triangle, and crease. Open flat.

*(c illustration)*

d. Bring C to B, forming triangle, and crease.

e. With triangle up, hold A/D between thumbs and forefingers at bottom edge of triangle. Push fingers toward center, forming four equal triangles.

f. Lay piece down on table with triangle up (two on each side) and crease firmly. *Note: At this point, choose which pattern you want to feature and make 17 pieces with the same design showing. To change the pattern, rotate the triangles around until you have chosen another pattern.*

g. With point down and long straight edge at the top, fold in half horizontally.

h. Picking up two triangle pieces from the left side, fold outside edges back to center line and crease. *Note: The tip will extend above the top straight edge.*

i. Repeat with remaining pieces.

j. To assemble, hold one piece in your left hand with single point down. Open right two pieces and using glue pen, place a dot of glue on back piece. Pick up a second piece in right hand and open the left two triangles. Slide top left triangle of second piece between the two open pieces in left hand.

k. Slide second piece up so that extended tips of piece in your left hand are even with center line. *Note: They should meet at the center of the V.*

l.  Continue adding pieces from the right until the circle is finished.

1

3.  Using bone folder, fold burgundy cardstock into thirds to create 3½" x 5½" tri-fold card. Refer to How do I fold cardstock? on page 18.

4.  Place card on cutting mat. Using circle cutter, cut 2¾"-diameter circle in center of first section of card.

5.  Place green cardstock on cutting mat, and cut a 3½"-diameter circle. Center and using glue pen, adhere circle onto back of third section of card. *Note: When the card is folded, the green will show through the hole on the front of the card.*

6.  Place a drop of glue on back of each point of sunburst design. Position on front of card evenly around edge of hole.

7.  Using glue stick, glue remaining 2" design square onto center of green circle. *Note: Make certain when the card is closed that the design is centered in the middle of the starburst.*

# How do I design a card with a confetti pocket?

Gently untie and loosen the thread at the top of this heart and dozens of wishes will be showered on the recipient. This is a wonderful way to send messages of love to a new baby, the bride and groom, or your spouse. The confetti is created by typing or handwriting words, and cutting them into individual pieces. Hope, dreams, love, forever, peace, and congratulations are just a few of the words that can be used to convey your confetti message.

## Confetti Heart Pocket Card

*Designed by Jill Dahlberg for Vanessa-Ann Collection*
Photo on page 78.

## Here's how:

1. Using bone folder, fold pink cardstock in half to form 5½" x 6" card. Refer to How do I fold cardstock? on page 18.

2. Mount pink polka-dot paper onto front of card with double-stick tape.

3. Fold pink vellum in half to form 5" square. Draw heart shape on vellum. Using deckle-edged scissors, cut out heart through double thickness of vellum.

4. Type or handwrite desired words on a sheet of printer paper. Using craft scissors, cut out individual words.

## What you need to get started:

Papers:
Cardstock:
  pink patterned (11" x 6")
Computer-printer paper
  (one sheet)
Patterned:
  lt. pink polka dot (10" sq.)
Vellum: lt. pink (10" x 5")

## Other Materials and Tools:
Bone folder
Computer/printer (optional)
Craft scissors
Deckle-edged scissors
Double-stick tape
Embroidery floss: pink
Needle

**What to Say:**

I LOVE YOU.
IT IS AS *SIMPLE* and *COMPLICATED* AS THAT.

5. Holding both hearts together and starting at upper right, loosely sew a running stitch around heart with two strands of pink floss. Stop when you have stitched a little over halfway around heart. Place confetti between vellum hearts and finish stitching to top. Tie floss into bow.

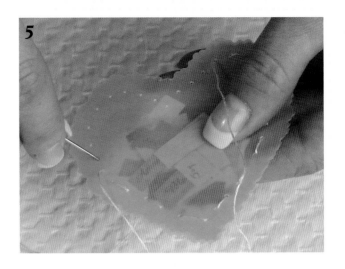

6. Mount heart onto front of card with two small pieces of double-stick tape.

*Designer's Note: You want the recipient to be able to remove the heart so he or she can pour out the confetti. Therefore, don't secure it too tightly.*

## Pocket Card Variation:

*Another romantic option for a pocket card can be created with an organdy "sandwich" of fringed fabric or two pieces of vellum. Stitch them, by hand or using a sewing machine, on three sides. Select and enclose three candy hearts with their sayings facing out when attached to the card. You can stitch the pocket to the card or dot glue with a glue gun to secure it to the card.*

## What you need to get started:

Papers:
Cardstock: white (10" x 5")

Other Materials and Tools:
Bone folder
Cardboard (1¾" x ¾")
Craft scissors
Fine-tipped marker: black
Glue pen
Hot-glue gun and glue sticks
Pearls (2" strand)
Ribbon roses: pink (5)
Seed beads: white (9)
Velvet fabric scrap, purple
   (2¾" x 1¾")

# How do I embellish a card with trims?

This is the perfect card for your special shopping partner, as a girl can never have too many purses. Pearls and roses embellish this cute purse, which is actually a small piece of cardboard wrapped with purple velvet. This is certain to bring a smile to any shopper.

## Embellished Purple Purse Card

*Designed by Jill Dahlberg for Vanessa-Ann Collection*

## Here's how:

1. Using bone folder, fold cardstock in half to form 5" square card. Refer to How do I fold cardstock? on page 18.

2. To make "purse," wrap purple velvet around cardboard and secure on back using glue gun. Adhere roses across top of purse. Cut one pearl from strand and adhere onto front of purse for button. Adhere pearl strand onto top of purse for handle. Adhere purse onto front of card.

3. Write "hello, girlfriend," below purse on front of card.

4. Using glue pen, randomly adhere beads over lower portion of card.

What to Say:

*A great deal of the feminine mystique can be attributed to the ancient art of accessorizing.*

hello, girlfriend

What to Say:

Take care of the luxuries and the
necessities will take care of themselves.

—Dorothy Parker

# How do I design a card, using corrugated paper?

This card appears very elegant with its white-on-white design. The corrugated paper offers a nice texture in contrast with the smooth vellum peaking through the window of the card. This would make a wonderful invitation to a wedding or anniversary party.

## *What you need to get started:*

Papers:
Corrugated: white (11" x 5½")
Vellum: white (11" x 5½")

Other Materials and Tools:
Bone folder
Craft knife
Cutting mat (or piece of thick cardboard)
Fine-tipped marker: white
Glue stick
Metal ruler
Pencil
Thin silver cord (18")

## Corrugated Window Card

*Designed by Jill Dahlberg for Vanessa-Ann Collection*

### *Here's how:*

1. Using bone folder, fold white corrugated paper in half to form 5½" square card. Refer to How do I fold cardstock? on page 18.

2. Draw 2¼" square on front of card.

3. Open up card so that you do not cut through both sides. Place card on cutting mat. Using metal ruler and craft knife, cut out square, creating a "window" in card front.

4. Fold white vellum in half to form 5½" square. Place vellum inside of card. Using glue stick, adhere vellum onto inside left and right. *Note: Only use glue stick in the corners, for a smooth appearance.*

5. With white pen, draw daisy on vellum window on front of card.

6. Tie silver cord around fold of card.

What to Say:

If I had a single flower for every time I think about you,
I could walk forever in my garden.

—Claudia Brandi

## What you need to get started:

Papers:
Cardstock: black (7¼" x 5½");
  plum (9½" sq.) (2" sq.);
  white (3½" sq.)
Vellum: metallic flecked
  (5¼" x 5")

Other Materials and Tools:
Bone folder
Computer/printer
  (optional)
Craft scissors
Double-stick tape
Kneaded eraser
Peel-and-stick adhesive sheet
Photograph (4¾" x 3½")
Photocopy machine
Silk variegated ribbon (21")
Soft-leaded pencil
Tracing paper

# How do I design a folded–envelope card?

This fun design is a card and an envelope all in one. It is a great way to send photographs to family and friends for an extra-special holiday greeting. Because it is its own envelope and is sealed on the back, it can safely be sent through the mail.

# Folded Envelope Card

*Designed by Bobbi Hill for Naptime Designs*

## Here's how:

1. Using a photocopy machine, enlarge the Envelope Pattern 200%. Using pencil, lightly transfer pattern fold lines, and markings onto tracing paper, then cut out pattern. Transfer patterns onto plum cardstock.

2. Cut out notches. Using bone folder, fold side in first then top and bottom. Refer to How do I fold cardstock? on page 18. If necessary, erase pencil markings.

3. Set the custom page size on your computer to match size of vellum. On plain paper, practice spacing your message so that it prints out on the lower third of page. When spacing is correct, run vellum through printer. *Note: The message can also be handwritten.*

4. Mount photo onto vellum with double-stick tape, then mount onto black cardstock.

5. Place a strip of double-stick tape across center back of photo card. Position across silk ribbon, leaving 7" tail on both sides. Mount onto inside-center of envelope card with double-stick tape.

6. Fold ribbon tails to center, then fold card, sides first.

7. Cut 2" square of peel-and-stick sheet and adhere onto 2" square of plum cardstock. Position over card flaps to seal.

Envelope Pattern

85

## What you need to get started:

**Papers:**
Cardstock: cream (8½" x 5½");
   white (3½" sq.)
Vellum: leaf green (3½" sq.)

**Other Materials and Tools:**
Bone folder
Christmas stickers, clear-
   backed: Christmas trees;
   snowman scene
Christmas sticker strips, clear-
   backed: Christmas lights
Craft scissors
Double-stick tape
Glitter glue
Organza ribbon:
   ⅜"-wide, red (8")
Porcelain ornament: oval (3")
Sheer ribbons:
   3"-wide, white (3")

# How do I design a card with a gift pocket?

Believe it or not, this quick and easy pocket card was made using stickers. The porcelain Christmas ornament looks as though it has been meticulously hand-painted; but it, too, is decorated with stickers. This is both a card and a gift. What a great idea for the many friends and neighbors on your Christmas list!

## Gift Pocket Holiday Card

*Designed by Stephanie Scheetz for Personal Stamp Exchange*

### Here's how:

1.  Using bone folder, fold cream cardstock in half to form 4¼" x 5½" card. Refer to How do I fold cardstock? on page 18.

2.  Adhere snowman stickers onto porcelain ornament. Tie on red ribbon for hanger. Embellish image with glitter glue, and set aside to dry.

3.  Attach sheer white ribbon to white cardstock on three sides with Christmas sticker strips.

4.  Angle and layer green square onto white ribbon square. Mount squares onto front of cream card with double-stick tape.

5.  Embellish card with Christmas tree stickers.

6.  When dry, place ornament in pocket.

*Designer's Note: The stickers used in this design were Snowman, Holiday Lights, and Small Tree by Personal Stamp Exchange. Be certain to choose stickers that have a clear background. This allows you to place them on any color of surface, and the surface will show through the sticker.*

**Papers:**
Cardstock: white (8½" x 4¼")
Mat board (2¼" sq.)
Vellum: lt. blue (4" sq.);
   lavender (3½" sq.)

**Other Materials and Tools:**
Archival pigment ink pad:
   violet
Batting (2" sq.)
Bone folder
Butterfly charm
Double-stick tape
Eyelets: lavender (4)
Industrial-strength glue
Lavender-scented oil
Pearlescent water-based paints:
   lt. blue; lavender; pink
Rubber stamp: hydrangea
Ruler
Silk fabric scrap:
   white (3½" sq.)
Sponge

# How do I design a sachet card?

The subtle scent of lavender added to this sachet makes this card one that the recipient will cherish for many days to come. It can be tucked into a drawer to delicately scent the contents, or placed on a desk as a gentle stress reliever. This card was created using rubber stamps on fabric, but purchased printed fabric will work just as well. The pearlescent paint adds a lovely shimmer to the fabric.

## Silk Pillow Sachet Card

*Designed by Stephanie Scheetz for Personal Stamp Exchange*

### Here's how:

1. Using wet sponge, gently dab pearlescent paint onto silk square. Let dry.

2. Ink hydrangea stamp with violet pad and stamp image onto silk square. Refer to Technique 12, Step 1a–c on pages 42–44.

3. Place batting over mat board. Add a few drops of lavender oil inside batting. *Note: Try to keep oil in inside batting so that it doesn't come in contact with the silk fabric.*

4. Wrap stamped silk over batting and secure to back of mat board with double-stick tape.

5. Using bone folder, fold white cardstock in half to form 4¼" square card. Refer to How do I fold cardstock? on page 18.

6. Attach blue vellum to front of card with eyelets.

7. Mount sachet onto purple vellum with double-stick tape. Gently tear around edges, leaving about ¼" border. Mount onto front of card with double-stick tape.

*Designer's Note: An additional design idea is to use a floral-print fabric to complement the color and type of the sachet, such as rose.*

8. Using industrial-strength glue, adhere butterfly charm onto sachet.

*Note: It is important when stamping on silk, or other glossy surfaces, to use an archival pigment ink pad. This special ink will not run. Heat-setting will speed up drying time.*

*Designer's Note: Personal Stamp Exchange suggests using Shimmerz™ as the pearlescent paint that is sponged onto the fabric. Because this is water-based and fast drying, it can be used in places that other types of paint cannot. It comes in many different colors; and can be used directly on a stamp, mixed with other inks, or painted on as a highlight.*

# 10
## project

### *What you need to get started:*

Papers:
Cardstock:
  sage green (4½" x 3½);
  white (8½" x 5½") (5" x 4")
Mat board: white (5" x 4")

Other Materials and Tools:
Bone folder
Christmas pinecone
Craft knife
Double-stick tape
Glitter beads: 5mm clear
  (1 pkg.)
Glue stick
Metal ruler
Peel-and-stick adhesive sheet
Photo corners: gold
Rubber stamps: country
Stamp pads: black
  (waterproof); metallic gold
Tray (to catch excess beads)
Watercolor markers or paints

# How do I design a card, using glitter beads?

This classic Christmas card gives the illusion of looking through a frosted glass window on a snowy day. This look is achieved by using a peel-and-stick adhesive sheet and tiny clear glitter beads. Although we used the technique over a stamped image, you could get the same effect by using a favorite image from a magazine or old greeting card.

# Glitter Bead Christmas Card

*Designed by Stephanie Scheetz for Personal Stamp Exchange*

## Here's how:

1. Ink country Christmas stamp with black pad, and stamp image on white cardstock. Refer to Technique 12, Step 1a–c on pages 42–44. Let dry.

2. Using watercolor markers or paints, color image as desired. Refer to Technique 12, Step 3 on page 44.

3. Using glue stick, adhere colored image onto mat board.

4. Place metal ruler along border of image. Using craft knife, trim all sides with craft knife.

5. Adhere peel-and-stick sheet over image. Expose adhesive and place image on tray.

6. Pour glitter beads over adhesive sheet until completely covered. Press to firmly adhere beads in place. Pour excess beads back into package.

7. Ink pinecone stamp with metallic-gold pad, and stamp randomly on sage-green cardstock. Attach gold photo corners to opposite corners of card.

8. Using bone folder, fold cream cardstock in half to form 5½" x 4¼" card. Refer to How do I fold cardstock? on page 18.

9. Using double-stick tape, angle and mount pinecone card onto front of cream card. Mount beaded image onto pinecone card in the same manner.

*Designer's Notes: Personal Stamp Exchange suggests using PeelnStick Sheet™ adhesive to adhere the beads. Some double-stick adhesives on the market are not tacky enough to hold the beads in place.*

*Whenever you plan to color the image with watercolor markers or paints, make certain to use a waterproof ink pad.*

## What you need to get started:

**Papers:**
Cardstock:
  cream (9" x 6¼");
  deep red (2" x 2");
  metallic silver (2¾" x 3")
Mulberry: black (3" x 6");
  royal blue (5" x 3")

**Other Materials and Tools:**
Bone folder
Craft scissors
Glue stick
Photo corners (2)
Postage stamp
Ruler
Thin silver cord (24")

# How do I design a card, using postage stamps?

Postage stamps are more than just a means to send a letter. There are hundreds of wonderful commemorative stamps that can be used as artwork. In this touching hero's tribute, the stamp is complemented with papers in a variety of colors and finishes, including photo corners. Choose paper that coordinates with the stamp you select. Embellishing your card with thin silver cord adds a rich touch.

# Postage Stamp
# Note Card

*Designed by Jill Dahlberg for Vanessa-Ann Collection*

## Here's how:

1.  Using bone folder, fold cream cardstock in half to form 4½" x 6¼" card. Refer to How do I fold cardstock? on page 18.

2.  Gently tear along 3" edges of black mulberry paper. Center and glue onto front of card. Refer to Technique 4, Step 3a–b on page 27.

3.  Adhere postage stamp onto royal-blue mulberry paper. Trim around stamp, leaving ¼" border.

4.  Mount this onto deep-red cardstock. Trim around edges, leaving ⅛" border.

5.  Attach photo corners to two corners and mount design onto royal-blue mulberry paper. Trim around edges, leaving a ½" border.

6.  Mount design onto metallic-silver cardstock. Trim around edges, leaving ⅛" border.

7.  Center and adhere layered stamp art onto black mulberry paper on front of card.

## Postage Stamp Variation:

*Layer and glue textured papers, contrasting mats, silver cord or metallic string, and a charming postage stamp onto the front of a card. Position the arrangement so that the image on the stamp appears to be framed or peeking out from its mat "window." Angle the cord or metallic string in a jaunty manner for a gift-like look.*

## What you need to get started:

Papers:
Cardstock: lt. brown (scrap);
    burgundy (9" x 5½")
Computer-printer paper
Newspaper cartoon

Other Materials and Tools:
Bone folder
Computer/printer
Craft scissors
Glue stick

# How do I design a collaged greeting card?

This collaged card was created using cardstock and an antique newspaper cartoon. Antique paper is not necessary for creating a collaged greeting card. Any type of paper, from tissue paper to wallpaper, can be used. Simply arrange papers as desired onto folded cardstock and let the fun begin.

# Collaged Card

*Designed by P. A. Gibbons for Fine Art Collage*

## Here's how:

1. Using the bone folder, fold burgundy cardstock in half to form 4½" x 5½" card. Refer to How do I fold cardstock? on page 18.

2. Cut around cartoon as desired.

3. Adhere the cartoon onto top portion of card.

4. Using computer printer, print out desired message, leaving enough space between each word to be cut apart.

5. Cut apart message and adhere onto card front below cartoon.

## Collage Variation:

*Using the idea of cut-out words, collect scraps of musical scores, gift wrap, stickers, and decals to glue onto a card. Create more interest by using two differently sized dark background shapes first, and then glue a pleasing arrangement of words and images so they overlap one another.*

What to Say:

We ate,
we drank,
we were merry . . .
Thank you for the hospitality.

## What you need to get started:

Papers:
Cardstock:
  pink gingham (4" x 12")
Patterned: baby rattles
Vellum: pink

Other Materials and Tools:
Bone folder
Craft scissors
Decorative-edged scissors:
  scalloped
Fine-tipped marker: metallic
  silver
Hole punch
Ruler
Satin ribbon: ½"-wide, pink

# How do I tie a folded design element onto a card?

Design elements can be attached to a greeting card in several ways. This "envelope and card in one" features a narrow satin ribbon as its means of attachment to the stiff cardstock that can stand. Ideal for a shower place card or favor, an invitation, or the centerpiece on a buffet table, this delightful card simply begs to be opened for its message.

# Ribbon-tied Card

*Designed by Jill Dahlberg for Vanessa-Ann Collection*

## Here's how:

1. Using the bone folder, fold pink gingham cardstock in half to form 4" x 6" card. Refer to How do I fold cardstock? on page 18.

2. Using decorative-edged scissors, scallop bottom edge of card.

3. Using Present Pattern at right, cut out design from patterned paper.

4. Fold in sides then top and bottom, creating a present. Write desired message on present.

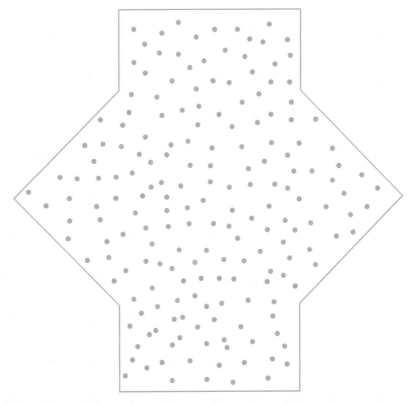

Present Pattern

5. Punch one hole 1" in from side and 2" down from top. Punch another hole 2" across from the first. *Note: The present should fit centered between the two holes.*

6. Thread ends of ribbon through holes from inside of card. Center present between the two holes. Tie ribbon around present and into a bow.

7. Using craft scissors, cut 2½" x ¾" rectangle from pink vellum.

8. Using the metallic-silver pen, write "Baby Shower" on rectangle and outline around edges.

9. Center and adhere onto bottom portion of card.

# How do I use corrugated cardboard to create a three-dimensional image?

## What you need to get started:

**Papers:**
Cardstock: white (8" x 6")
Corrugated cardboard:
   brown (2¼" sq.)
Mulberry: rust (2¼" sq.)
Text from real estate section of
   newspaper

**Other Materials and Tools:**
Bone folder
Craft scissors
Fine-tipped marker: red
Glue stick
Paint pen: metallic gold

Corrugated cardboard can be a great way to add dimension to an image. In this project, it is used to make a "sign." Using this same technique, you can make signs for many occasions—passing a test or driver's exam, going off to college, or celebrating a new job or pet.

## Corrugated Cardboard Card

*Designed by Anneliese Oughton for Anni's Attic*

## Here's how:

1. Using bone folder, fold cardstock in half to form 4" x 6" card. Refer to How do I fold cardstock? on page 18.

2. Cut out small house shape from newspaper. Using red marker, write "SOLD" diagonally across house.

3. Tear around edges of mulberry paper. Refer to Technique 4, Step 3a–b on page 27. Using glue stick, adhere and mount mulberry paper onto corrugated cardboard. Adhere house onto mulberry paper, and mount entire piece onto front of card.

4. Using metallic-gold paint pen, draw border around edge of corrugated image. Add a small circle and two lines at the top to give the impression of a framed picture hanging on a wall. Write "NEW HOME" under picture.

NEW HOME

What to Say:

Every house where love abides and friendship is a guest, is surely home, and home sweet home for there the heart can rest.

## What you need to get started:

**Papers:**
Cardstock: black (5½" x 11")
  (5" sq.) (2½" sq.) (2" sq.)
Wallpaper:
  black/gold (4½" sq.)

**Other Materials and Tools:**
Bone folder
Craft scissors
Embossing heat tool
Embossing powder:
  metallic gold
Glue stick
Pigment ink embossing pad
Rubber stamp: oriental
  character

# How do I design a card, using wallpaper?

Wallpaper's unique texture adds dimension to a greeting card. Use scraps of wallpaper just like any other kind of paper for embellishment. With the large variety of wallpaper available the possibilities are endless.

## Oriental Wallpaper Card

*Designed by Chris Kamens for Neetztuff*

### Here's how:

1.  Using bone folder, fold cardstock to form 5½" square card. Refer to How do I fold cardstock? on page 18.

2.  Using metallic-gold pen, outline edges of 5" square, 2½" square, and 2" square.

3.  Using glue stick, center and adhere wallpaper onto 5" square.

4.  Press rubber stamp onto embossing ink pad.

5.  Stamp onto 2" square. Refer to Technique 12, Step 1a–c on pages 42–44.

6.  Heat-emboss with metallic-gold powder. Refer to Technique 13, Step 4a–b on page 47.

7.  Center and adhere 5" square onto card. Center and adhere wallpaper square onto 5" square. Adhere 2½" square in upper right-hand corner of wallpaper square. Center and adhere embossed 2" square onto 2½" square.

Good friends,
   good times,
      good memories.
         Thanks!

**What to Say:**

**What to Say:**

*When we give cheerfully and accept graciously, everyone is blessed.*

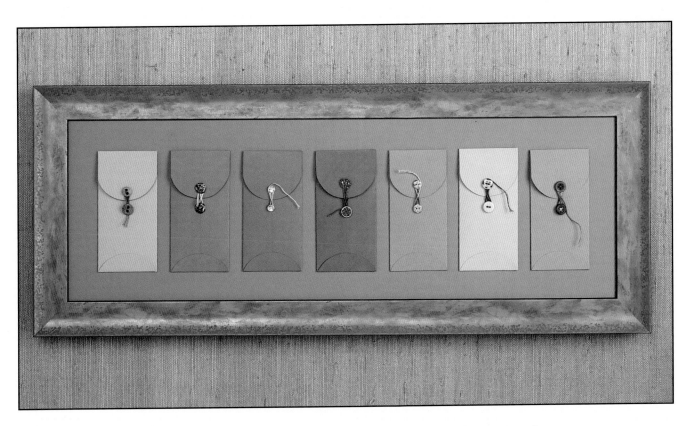

# Section 4: creative presentations

103

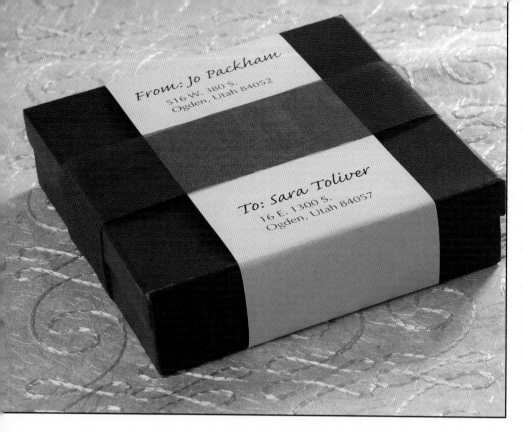

A box can actually be the envelope that a card, letter, or invitation is sent in. Place the card directly inside the box, include confetti or a small ornament-style gift, and send. If the paper and ribbons are glued down these can actually go through the mail this way. Be certain to allow space below the address for the bar code sticker the postal service will affix. The receiver of such a boxed card will no doubt be delighted by such an elegant presentation.

Oriental cards and envelopes can be handmade using natural materials. A small square of paper and a twig are adhered to the envelope flap, then gold thread is wound around the twig and is used to wrap the envelope and keep it closed.

Messages, invitations, and love letters can be given or sent in a translucent bottle. Simply create your message or invitation on parchment or vellum, roll it like a scroll, tie with a ribbon, and insert into a bottle. If possible, select a bottle with an unusual shape. A unique stopper—perhaps one with a gem-like appearance—is especially lovely. There are innumerable ways to create extra charm with ties, tags, and trinket enclosures. You can even scent the paper with a dab of perfume.

To make the occasion even more special, attach a tag to the outside of the bottle. If this style of bottled message is to be sent through the postal service make certain that the bottle is well protected in a small box.

Have part of your message include a small "gift" that is mentioned in the copy of the card. In this example a small red wagon is found inside the box with the card and the envelope—to help the receiver know that "wishes do come true!"

From: Amy Booth
200 W. State St.
Bountiful, Utah 84123

To: Tracey Rydalch
153 W. Gentile St.
Layton, Utah 84021

To: Kim Taylor
1532 E. 3rd Ave.
Salt Lake City, Utah 84111

Cans can be used as "envelopes" and actually sent through the mail. Write or type your information on the label, adhere the paper labels to the can with permanent (not repositionable) spray adhesive, and send through the mail. The invitation, card, or letter can be rolled and placed directly inside of the can. Include confetti or small trinkets along with the invitation, before securing the lid.

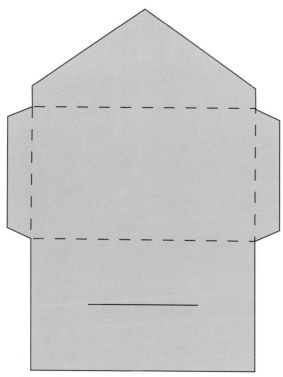

Pattern for a Basic Envelope

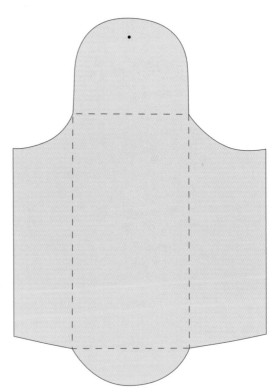

Narrow Clasp Envelope shown above

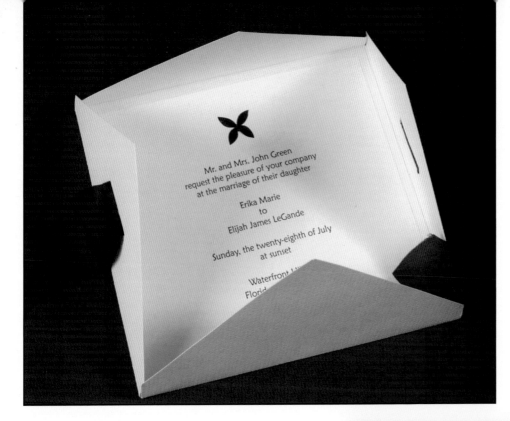

Cards that are envelopes serve as "self-mailers" with the message inside. Vellum or parchment for the words or an overlay on top of them makes an elegant style statement when the card is opened. Embellish with appliqués, stamp art, or watercolor accents. Ribbon closures threaded through the slits can be color co-ordinated with a two-tone cardstock. The envelopes featured on this page were created by Envelopments®.

Envelopes can be made in a variety of shapes and sizes. The patterns at the left provide you with two types of envelopes. *Note: To determine the size of your card, measure the center area of the envelope between the fold lines. The card should be cut ½" smaller on all sides.* Simply enlarge pattern to desired size. Crease and fold on dotted lines. Using a glue stick, seal the bottom and sides. The top envelope flap can be sealed with a clasp, such as the two-button clasp as shown in the photo at the left, or with stickers, ribbons, wax, or double-stick tape.

# Acknowledgments

The following people/companies provided some of the cards and/or products for this book. We would like to thank them for their participation.

LuAnn Vermillion
for Wildflowers by LuAnn
www.wildflowersbyluann.com

Sandi Genovese
for Ellison®
www.ellison.com

Anneliese Oughton
for Anni's Attic
www.annisattic.com

Bonnie Eisenberg,
Stephanie Scheetz
Jennifer Lynch
for Personal Stamp Exchange
www.psxdesign.com

Laura Lees
for L. Paper Designs
www.lpaperdesigns.com

P. A. Gibbons
for Fine Art Collage
www.pagibbons.com

Chris Kamens
for Neetztuff
www.neetztuff.com

Joyleene Abrey
for Snowflake Cards
www.snowflakecards.co.uk

Lorilyn Tenney
e-mail: MrsTeny@aol.com

Jill Dahlberg
Jo Packham
Sara Toliver
for Vannessa-Ann Collection
Ogden, UT

Envelopments®
www.envelopments.com

# Metric Equivalency Chart

inches to millimetres and centimetres (mm-millimetres  cm-centimetres)

| inches | mm | cm | inches | cm | inches | cm | inches | cm |
|--------|----|----|--------|-----|--------|-----|--------|-----|
| ⅛ | 3 | 0.3 | 6 | 15.2 | 21 | 53.3 | 36 | 91.4 |
| ¼ | 6 | 0.6 | 7 | 17.8 | 22 | 55.9 | 37 | 94.0 |
| ⅜ | 10 | 1.0 | 8 | 20.3 | 23 | 58.4 | 38 | 96.5 |
| ½ | 13 | 1.3 | 9 | 22.9 | 24 | 61.0 | 39 | 99.1 |
| ⅝ | 16 | 1.6 | 10 | 25.4 | 25 | 63.5 | 40 | 101.6 |
| ¾ | 19 | 1.9 | 11 | 27.9 | 26 | 66.0 | 41 | 104.1 |
| ⅞ | 22 | 2.2 | 12 | 30.5 | 27 | 68.6 | 42 | 106.7 |
| 1 | 25 | 2.5 | 13 | 33.0 | 28 | 71.1 | 43 | 109.2 |
| 1¼ | 32 | 3.2 | 14 | 35.6 | 29 | 73.7 | 44 | 111.8 |
| 1½ | 38 | 3.8 | 15 | 38.1 | 30 | 76.2 | 45 | 114.3 |
| 1¾ | 44 | 4.4 | 16 | 40.6 | 31 | 78.7 | 46 | 116.8 |
| 2 | 51 | 5.1 | 17 | 43.2 | 32 | 81.3 | 47 | 119.4 |
| 3 | 76 | 7.6 | 18 | 45.7 | 33 | 83.8 | 48 | 121.9 |
| 4 | 102 | 10.2 | 19 | 48.3 | 34 | 86.4 | 49 | 124.5 |
| 5 | 127 | 12.7 | 20 | 50.8 | 35 | 88.9 | 50 | 127.0 |

# Index